D0515411

Introduction

Mathematical Thinking at Grade 2

Grade 2

Karen Economopoulos

Joan Akers

Doug Clements

Anne Goodrow

Jerrie Moffet

Julie Sarama

Developed at TERC, Cambridge, Massachusetts

Dale Seymour Publications®
White Plains, New York

The *Investigations* curriculum was developed at TERC (formerly
Technical Education Research Centers) in collaboration with Kent State
University and the State University of New York at Buffalo. The work was
supported in part by National Science Foundation Grant No. ESI-9050210.
TERC is a nonprofit company working to improve mathematics and science
education. TERC is located at 2067 Massachusetts Avenue, Cambridge,
MA 02140.

**This project was supported, in part,
by the**
National Science Foundation
Opinions expressed are those of the authors
and not necessarily those of the Foundation

Managing Editor: Catherine Anderson
Grade-Level Editor: Alison Abrohms
Series Editor: Beverly Cory
Revision Team: Laura Marshall Alavosus, Ellen Harding, Patty Green Holubar,
Suzanne Knott, Beverly Hersh Lozoff
ESL Consultant: Nancy Sokol Green
Production/Manufacturing Director: Janet Yearian
Production/Manufacturing Coordinator: Amy Changar, Shannon Miller
Design Manager: Jeff Kelly
Design: Don Taka
Illustrations: Meryl Treatner, Laurie Harden
Cover: Bay Graphics
Composition: Archetype Book Composition

This book is published by Dale Seymour Publications®, an imprint of
Addison Wesley Longman, Inc.

> Dale Seymour Publications
> 10 Bank Street
> White Plains, NY 10602
> Customer Service 1-800-872-1100

Order number DS43800
ISBN 1-57232-653-0
      7 8 9 10-ML-02 01 00

 Printed on Recycled Paper

INVESTIGATIONS IN NUMBER, DATA, AND SPACE®

T E R C

Principal Investigator   Susan Jo Russell

Co-Principal Investigator   Cornelia Tierney

Director of Research and Evaluation   Jan Mokros

Director of K–2 Curriculum   Karen Economopoulos

Curriculum Development
Joan Akers
Michael T. Battista
Mary Berle-Carman
Douglas H. Clements
Karen Economopoulos
Anne Goodrow
Marlene Kliman
Jerrie Moffett
Megan Murray
Ricardo Nemirovsky
Andee Rubin
Susan Jo Russell
Cornelia Tierney
Tracey Wright

Evaluation and Assessment
Mary Berle-Carman
Jan Mokros
Andee Rubin

Teacher Support
Anne Goodrow
Liana Laughlin
Jerrie Moffett
Megan Murray
Tracey Wright

Technology Development
Michael T. Battista
Douglas H. Clements
Julie Sarama

Video Production
David A. Smith
Judy Storeygard

Administration and Production
Irene Baker
Amy Catlin
Amy Taber

**Cooperating Classrooms
for This Unit**
Rose Christiansen
*Brookline Public Schools
Brookline, MA*

Lisa Seyferth
Carol Walker
*Newton Public Schools
Newton, MA*

Phyllis Ollove
*Boston Public Schools
Boston, MA*

Margaret M. McGaffigan
*Nashoba Regional School District
Stow, MA*

Pat Chartier
Marina Seevak
*Cambridge Public Schools
Cambridge, MA*

Barbara Rynerson
Dale Dhoore
Beth Newkirk
Pat McLure
*Oyster River Public Schools
Durham, NH*

Consultants and Advisors
Deborah Lowenberg Ball
Marilyn Burns
Ann Grady
James J. Kaput
Mary M. Lindquist
John Olive
Leslie P. Steffe
Grayson Wheatley

Graduate Assistants
Kathryn Battista
Caroline Borrow
Judy Norris
Kent State University

Julie Sarama
Sudha Swaminathan
Elaine Vukelic
State University of New York at Buffalo

Revisions and Home Materials
Cathy Miles Grant
Marlene Kliman
Margaret McGaffigan
Megan Murray
Kim O'Neil
Andee Rubin
Susan Jo Russell
Lisa Seyferth
Myriam Steinback
Judy Storeygard
Anna Suarez
Cornelia Tierney
Carol Walker
Tracey Wright

CONTENTS

TEACHER NOTES

WHERE TO START

The first-time user of *Mathematical Thinking at Grade 2* should read the following:

When you next teach this same unit, you can begin to read more of the background. Each time you present the unit, you will learn more about how your students understand the mathematical ideas.

Investigations in Number, Data, and Space® is a K–5 mathematics curriculum with four major goals:

- to offer students meaningful mathematical problems
- to emphasize depth in mathematical thinking rather than superficial exposure to a series of fragmented topics
- to communicate mathematics content and pedagogy to teachers
- to substantially expand the pool of mathematically literate students

The *Investigations* curriculum embodies a new approach based on years of research about how children learn mathematics. Each grade level consists of a set of separate units, each offering 2–8 weeks of work. These units of study are presented through investigations that involve students in the exploration of major mathematical ideas.

Approaching the mathematics content through investigations helps students develop flexibility and confidence in approaching problems, fluency in using mathematical skills and tools to solve problems, and proficiency in evaluating their solutions. Students also build a repertoire of ways to communicate about their mathematical thinking, while their enjoyment and appreciation of mathematics grows.

The investigations are carefully designed to invite all students into mathematics—girls and boys, members of diverse cultural, ethnic, and language groups, and students with different strengths and interests. Problem contexts often call on students to share experiences from their family, culture, or community. The curriculum eliminates barriers—such as work in isolation from peers, or emphasis on speed and memorization—that exclude some students from participating successfully in mathematics. The following aspects of the curriculum ensure that all students are included in significant mathematics learning:

- Students spend time exploring problems in depth.
- They find more than one solution to many of the problems they work on.

- They invent their own strategies and approaches, rather than rely on memorized procedures.
- They choose from a variety of concrete materials and appropriate technology, including calculators, as a natural part of their everyday mathematical work.
- They express their mathematical thinking through drawing, writing, and talking.
- They work in a variety of groupings—as a whole class, individually, in pairs, and in small groups.
- They move around the classroom as they explore the mathematics in their environment and talk with their peers.

While reading and other language activities are typically given a great deal of time and emphasis in elementary classrooms, mathematics often does not get the time it needs. If students are to experience mathematics in depth, they must have enough time to become engaged in real mathematical problems. We believe that a minimum of 5 hours of mathematics classroom time a week—about an hour a day—is critical at the elementary level. The scope and pacing of the *Investigations* curriculum are based on that belief.

We explain more about the pedagogy and principles that underlie these investigations in Teacher Notes throughout the units. For correlations of the curriculum to the NCTM Standards and further help in using this research-based program for teaching mathematics, see the following books, available from Dale Seymour Publications:

- *Implementing the* Investigations in Number, Data, and Space® *Curriculum*
- *Beyond Arithmetic: Changing Mathematics in the Elementary Classroom* by Jan Mokros, Susan Jo Russell, and Karen Economopoulos

This book is one of the curriculum units for *Investigations in Number, Data, and Space*. In addition to providing part of a complete mathematics curriculum for your students, this unit offers information to support your own professional development. You, the teacher, are the person who will make this curriculum come alive in the classroom; the book for each unit is your main support system.

Although the curriculum does not include student textbooks, reproducible sheets for student work are provided in the unit and are also available as Student Activity Booklets. Students work actively with objects and experiences in their own environment and with a variety of manipulative materials and technology, rather than with a book of instruction and problems. We strongly recommend use of the overhead projector as a way to present problems, to focus group discussion, and to help students share ideas and strategies.

Ultimately, every teacher will use these investigations in ways that make sense for his or her particular style, the particular group of students, and the constraints and supports of a particular school environment. Each unit offers information and guidance for a wide variety of situations, drawn from our collaborations with many teachers and students over many years. Our goal in this book is to help you, a professional educator, implement this curriculum in a way that will give all your students access to mathematical power.

Investigation Format

The opening two pages of each investigation help you get ready for the work that follows.

What Happens This gives a synopsis of each session or block of sessions.

Mathematical Emphasis This lists the most important ideas and processes students will encounter in this investigation.

What to Plan Ahead of Time These lists alert you to materials to gather, sheets to duplicate, transparencies to make, and anything else you need to do before starting.

INVESTIGATION 2

Looking at Numbers

What Happens

Session 1: How Many Days Have We Been in School? Students are introduced to the routine, Today's Number, which will be incorporated into their school day throughout the year. They begin a class counting strip that represents the number of days they have been in school. They also record these data on a 200 chart. Students find various ways to express Today's Number using arithmetic operations.

Sessions 2 and 3: Card Games Students play two card games, Tens Go Fish and Turn Over 10. They are introduced to Choice Time activities, which they participate in for the rest of the sessions.

Sessions 4 and 5: Mystery Photos Students are introduced to two new activities, Mystery Photos and Building Cube Things. They work on these activities during Choice Time.

Session 6: Today's Number and Counting Pockets In the first half of this session, students brainstorm ways to express the number of days they have been in school. During the last half of the session, students are introduced to How Many Pockets?, the second of three ongoing classroom routines. They collect data about the number of pockets the class is wearing.

Session 7: Revealing Mystery Photos Students continue the Choice Time activities they worked on in Sessions 2–5. At the end of the session, they reveal the Mystery Photo locations and have a brief discussion about Choice Time.

Session 8: Ways to Get to 12 The book *12 Ways to Get to 11* is read to the class. Students write number sentences and identify categories for some of the situations in the book. As a class, they write and illustrate a book based on the literature,

which expresses Today's Number in a variety of ways. For homework, they choose a different number and make their own "miniversion" of a book.

Mathematical Emphasis

■ Keeping track of the number of school days

■ Writing equations that equal the number of days in school

■ Making combinations of 10

■ Identifying uses of numbers in the world

INVESTIGATION 2

What to Plan Ahead of Time

Materials

■ Index cards and adding-machine tape (Session 1)

■ Interlocking cubes: at least 30 per student (Sessions 2–6)

■ Resealable plastic bags or envelopes to store Mystery Photo Cards and class sets of number cards: 2 per student (Sessions 2–5)

■ Chart paper or newsprint (Sessions 1, 6, 8)

■ Overhead projector (Sessions 4–5)

■ Large jar (Session 6)

■ Masking or colored tape, or a rubber band that fits the jar (Session 6)

■ *12 Ways to Get to 11* by Eve Merriam (Session 8, optional)

■ Plain paper: 2 sheets per student (Sessions 2–3, 6, 8)

Other Preparation

■ Duplicate the following student sheets and teaching resources (located at the end of this unit) in the following quantities. If you have Student Activity Booklets, copy only the items marked with an asterisk.

For Session 1
Student Sheet 4, How Do You Use Numbers? (p. 178): 1 per student (homework)

For Sessions 2–3
Student Sheet 5, Tens Go Fish (p. 179) and Student Sheet 6, Turn Over 10 (p. 180): 1 per student (homework), plus 6–7 for the classroom.*

For Sessions 4–5
Student Sheet 7, Mystery Photo Recording Sheet (p. 181): 1 per student
Student Sheet 8, Cube Things (p. 182): 1 per pair. Cut each sheet in half.

Mystery Photo Cards* (p. 190): 6 sets, plus overhead transparencies of three or four. Cut apart the sets and store each set in an envelope or resealable plastic bag.

For Session 6
Student Sheet 9, Pockets at Home (p. 183): 1 per student (homework)

For Session 8
Student Sheet 10, Ways to Get to _____ (p. 184): 1 per student (homework)

■ Prepare a blank 200 chart by taping together two copies of the 100 chart, one above the other to form a 10-by-20 grid. Post it in a permanent place on a bulletin board or mount it on a piece of cardboard. The chart will be used throughout the year to count the number of days in school. (Session 1)

■ Prepare Number of the Day cards using index cards that have been cut in half. Cut a paper strip from adding-machine tape, long enough to hold 180 number cards. Plan enough space to display the strip. (Session 1)

■ If you do not have manufactured number cards from the grade 2 *Investigations* materials kit, use Number Cards (p. 186) to make one deck of number cards per pair of students for classwork. The classroom decks will last longer if duplicated on oaktag. These sets can be cut apart and stored in envelopes or plastic bags. Also duplicate enough to provide one deck per student for homework. Each deck should contain four of each number 0–10 and four wild cards. See the Materials lists with specific activities to determine whether wild cards should be included with decks each time. (Sessions 2–3)

Sessions Within an investigation, the activities are organized by class session, a session being at least a one-hour math class. Sessions are numbered consecutively through an investigation. Often several sessions are grouped together, presenting a block of activities with a single major focus.

When you find a block of sessions presented together—for example, Sessions 1, 2, and 3—read through the entire block first to understand the overall flow and sequence of the activities. Make some preliminary decisions about how you will divide the activities into three sessions for your class, based on what you know about your students. You may need to modify your initial plans as you progress through the activities, and you may want to make notes in the margins of the pages as reminders for the next time you use the unit.

Be sure to read the Session Follow-Up section at the end of the session block to see what homework assignments and extensions are suggested as you make your initial plans.

While you may be used to a curriculum that tells you exactly what each class session should cover, we have found that the teacher is in a better position to make these decisions. Each unit is flexible and may be handled somewhat differently by every teacher. Although we provide guidance for how many sessions a particular group of activities is likely to need, we want you to be active in determining an appropriate pace and the best transition points for your class. It is not unusual for a teacher to spend more or less time than is proposed for the activities.

Classroom Routines The Start-Up at the beginning of each session offers suggestions for how to acknowledge and integrate homework from the previous session, and which Classroom Routine activities to include sometime during the school day. Routines provide students with regular practice in important mathematical skills such as solving number combinations, collecting and organizing data, understanding time, and seeing spatial relationships. Two routines, How Many Pockets? and Today's Number, are used regularly in the grade 2 *Investigations* units. A third routine, Time and Time Again, appears in the final unit, *Timelines and Rhythm Patterns*. This routine provides a variety of activities about understanding

---

Sessions 2 and 3

Card Games

Materials

- Number Cards, see specific activities as to whether to include wild cards (1 deck per pair, 1 deck per student, homework)
- Envelopes or resealable plastic bags (1 per student)
- Student Sheet 5 (1 per student, homework, plus 6–7 for the classroom)
- Student Sheet 6 (1 per student, homework, plus 6–7 for the classroom)
- Plain paper (2 sheets per person)
- Interlocking cubes

What Happens

Students play two card games, Tens Go Fish and Turn Over 10. They are introduced to Choice Time activities, which they participate in for the rest of the sessions. Their work focuses on:

- making 10 with two or more addends
- comparing two quantities and finding the difference
- counting a set of objects
- counting two sets of objects

Start-Up

Uses of Numbers Students share the uses of numbers they discussed with their families for homework. Add the new uses to the list started yesterday.

Today's Number Sometime during the school day, students brainstorm ways to express the number of days they have been in school. They add a card to the class counting strip and fill in another number on the blank 200 chart. For full directions on this routine, see p. 124.

Activity

Tens Go Fish

Tens Go Fish and Turn Over 10 are two card games that reinforce combinations of 10 with two or more addends. These can be taught to the whole class, or you might want to teach a small group of students and then have them teach other students. Try to teach both of these games during the first half of Session 2. These are two choice activities for students to work on during the remainder of Session 2 and all of Session 3.

Note: If you have duplicated the Number Cards on paper instead of card stock, have students make a "card holder" so they won't be able to see through the cards. Fold one long edge of a sheet of 8½"-by-11" paper up approximately 1 inch from the bottom to form a "pocket." Then fold the paper in half the long way, matching the bottom of the pocket with the other long edge. The paper can stand, forming a tent. Staple each side of the pocket. Slide cards into the pocket.

26 ▪ *Investigation 2: Looking at Numbers*

---

time; these can be easily integrated throughout the school day and into other parts of the classroom curriculum. A fourth routine, Quick Images, supports work in the unit *Shapes, Halves, and Symmetry*. After its introduction, you might do it once or twice a week to develop students' visual sense of number (as displayed in dot arrangements).

Most Classroom Routine activities are short and can be done whenever you have a spare 10 minutes—maybe before lunch or recess, or at the beginning or end of the day. Complete descriptions of the Classroom Routines can be found at the end of the units.

Activities The activities include pair and small-group work, individual tasks, and whole-class discussions. In any case, students are seated together, talking and sharing ideas during all work times. Students most often work cooperatively, although each student may record work individually.

Choice Time In most units, some sessions are structured with activity choices. In these cases, students may work simultaneously on different activities focused on the same mathematical ideas.

Students choose which activities they want to do, and they cycle through them.

You will need to decide how to set up and introduce these activities and how to let students make their choices. Some teachers set up choices as stations around the room, while others post the list of available choices and allow students to collect their own materials and choose their own work space. You may need to experiment with a few different structures before finding a set up that works best for you, your students, and your classroom.

Tips for the Linguistically Diverse Classroom At strategic points in each unit, you will find concrete suggestions for simple modifications of the teaching strategies to encourage the participation of all students. Many of these tips offer alternative ways to elicit critical thinking from students at varying levels of English proficiency, as well as from other students who find it difficult to verbalize their thinking.

The tips are supported by suggestions for specific vocabulary work to help ensure that all students can participate fully in the investigations. The Preview for the Linguistically Diverse Classroom lists important words that are assumed as part of the working vocabulary of the unit. Second-language learners will need to become familiar with these words in order to understand the problems and activities they will be doing. These terms can be incorporated into students' second-language work before or during the unit. Activities that can be used to present the words are found in the appendix, Vocabulary Support for Second-Language Learners. In addition, ideas for making connections to students' languages and cultures, included on the Preview page, help the class explore the unit's concepts from a multicultural perspective.

Session Follow-Up: Homework In *Investigations,* homework is an extension of classroom work. Sometimes it offers review and practice of work done in class, sometimes preparation for upcoming activities, and sometimes numerical practice that revisits work in earlier units. Homework plays a role both in supporting students' learning and in helping inform families about the ways in which students in this curriculum work with mathematical ideas.

Depending on your school's homework policies and your own judgment, you may want to assign more homework than is suggested in the units. For this purpose you might use the practice pages, included as blackline masters at the end of this unit, to give students additional work with numbers.

For some homework assignments, you will want to adapt the activity to meet the needs of a variety of students in your class: those with special needs, those ready for more challenge, and second-language learners. You might change the numbers in a problem, make the activity more or less complex, or go through a sample activity with those who need extra help. You can modify any student sheet for either homework or class use. In particular, making numbers in a problem smaller or larger can make the same basic activity appropriate for a wider range of students.

Another issue to consider is how to handle the homework that students bring back to class—how to recognize the work they have done at home without spending too much time on it. Some teachers hold a short group discussion of different approaches to the assignment; others ask students to share and discuss their work with a neighbor; still others post the homework around the room

and give students time to tour it briefly. If you want to keep track of homework students bring in, be sure it ends up in a designated place.

Session Follow-Up: Extensions Sometimes in Session Follow-Up, you will find suggested extension activities. These are opportunities for some or all students to explore a topic in greater depth or in a different context. They are not designed for "fast" students; mathematics is a multifaceted discipline, and different students will want to go further in different investigations. Look for and encourage the sparks of interest and enthusiasm you see in your students, and use the extensions to help them pursue these interests.

Excursions Some of the *Investigations* units include excursions—blocks of activities that could be omitted without harming the integrity of the unit. This is one way of dealing with the great depth and variety of elementary mathematics— much more than a class has time to explore in any one year. Excursions give you the flexibility to make different choices from year to year, doing the excursion in one unit this time, and next year trying another excursion.

Materials

A complete list of the materials needed for teaching this unit follows the unit overview. Some of these materials are available in kits for the *Investigations* curriculum. Individual items can also be purchased from school supply dealers.

Classroom Materials In an active mathematics classroom, certain basic materials should be available at all times: interlocking cubes, pencils, unlined paper, graph paper, calculators, and things to count with. Some activities in this curriculum require scissors and glue sticks or tape. Stick-on notes and large paper are also useful materials throughout.

So that students can independently get what they need at any time, they should know where these materials are kept, how they are stored, and how they are to be returned to the storage area. Many teachers have found that stopping 5 minutes before the end of each session so that students can finish their work and clean up is helpful in maintaining classroom materials. You'll find that establishing such routines at the beginning of the year is well worth the time and effort.

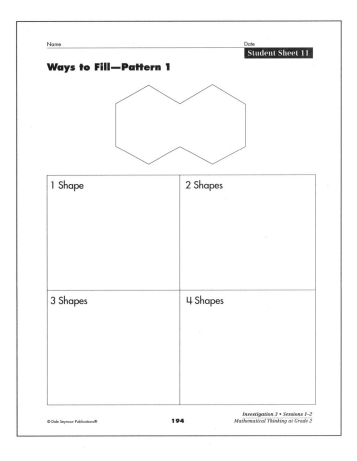

Student Sheets and Teaching Resources Student recording sheets and other teaching tools needed for both class and homework are provided as reproducible blackline masters at the end of each unit.

We think it's important that students find their own ways of organizing and recording their work. They need to learn how to explain their thinking with both drawings and written words, and how to organize their results so someone else can understand them. For this reason, we deliberately do not provide student sheets for every activity. Regardless of the form in which students do their work, we recommend that they keep their work in a mathematics folder, notebook, or journal so that it is always available to them for reference.

Student Activity Booklets These booklets contain all the sheets each student will need for individual work, freeing you from extensive copying (although you may need or want to copy the occasional teaching resource on transparency film or card stock, or make extra copies of a student sheet).

Computers and Calculators Calculators are introduced to students in the second unit of the grade 2 sequence, *Coins, Coupons, and Combinations*. It is assumed that calculators are readily available throughout the curriculum.

Computer activities are offered at all grade levels. Although the software is linked to activities in three units in grade 2, we recommend that students use it throughout the year. As students use the software over time, they continue to develop skills presented in the units. How you incorporate the computer activities into your curriculum depends on the number of computers you have available. Technology in the Curriculum discusses ways to incorporate the use of calculators and computers into classroom activities.

Children's Literature Each unit offers a list of related children's literature that can be used to support the mathematical ideas in the unit. Sometimes an activity is based on a selected children's book, with suggestions for substitutions where practical. While such activities can be adapted and taught without the book, the literature offers a rich introduction and should be used whenever possible.

Investigations at **Home** It is a good idea to make your policy on homework explicit to both students and their families when you begin teaching with *Investigations*. How frequently will you be assigning homework? When do you expect homework to be completed and brought back to school? What are your goals in assigning homework? How independent should families expect their children to be? What should the parent's or guardian's role be? The more explicit you can be about your expectations, the better the homework experience will be for everyone.

Investigations at Home (a booklet available separately for each unit, to send home with students) gives you a way to communicate with families about the work students are doing in class. This booklet includes a brief description of every session, a list of the mathematics content emphasized in each investigation, and a discussion of each homework assignment to help families more effectively support their children. Whether or not you are using the *Investigations* at Home booklets, we

expect you to make your own choices about homework assignments. Feel free to omit any and to add extra ones you think are appropriate.

Family Letter A letter that you can send home to students' families is included with the blackline masters for each unit. Families need to be informed about the mathematics work in your classroom; they should be encouraged to participate in and support their children's work. A reminder to send home the letter for each unit appears in one of the early investigations. These letters are also available separately in Spanish, Vietnamese, Cantonese, Hmong, and Cambodian.

Help for You, the Teacher

Because we believe strongly that a new curriculum must help teachers think in new ways about mathematics and about their students' mathematical thinking processes, we have included a great deal of material to help you learn more about both.

About the Mathematics in This Unit This introductory section summarizes the critical informa-

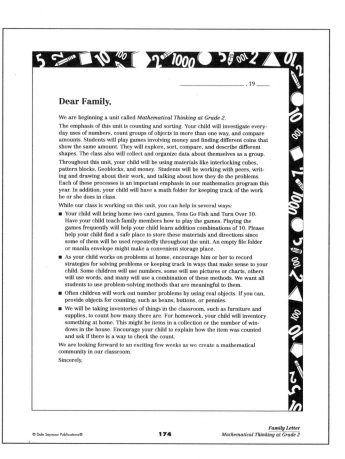

tion about the mathematics you will be teaching. It describes the unit's central mathematical ideas and the ways students will encounter them through the unit's activities.

About the Assessment in This Unit This introductory section highlights Teacher Checkpoints and assessment activities contained in the unit. It offers questions to stimulate your assessment as you observe the development of students' mathematical thinking and learning.

Teacher Notes These reference notes provide practical information about the mathematics you are teaching and about our experience with how students learn. Many of the notes were written in response to actual questions from teachers or to discuss important things we saw happening in the field-test classrooms. Some teachers like to read them all before starting the unit, then review them as they come up in particular investigations.

Dialogue Boxes Sample dialogues demonstrate how students typically express their mathematical

ideas, what issues and confusions arise in their thinking, and how some teachers have guided class discussions.

These dialogues are based on the extensive classroom testing of this curriculum; many are word-for-word transcriptions of recorded class discussions. They are not always easy reading; sometimes it may take some effort to unravel what the students are trying to say. But this is the value of these dialogues; they offer good clues to how your students may develop and express their approaches and strategies, helping you prepare for your own class discussions.

Where to Start You may not have time to read everything the first time you use this unit. As a first-time user, you will likely focus on understanding the activities and working them out with your students. Read completely through all the activities before starting to present them. Also read those sections listed in the Contents under the heading Where to Start.

Encouraging Thinking and Reasoning ⟨Teacher Note⟩

The student's role in math class is an active one. Getting correct answers is not enough; students should be encouraged to think critically about their ideas, give reasons for their answers, and communicate their ideas to others. Reflecting on one's own thinking and learning is a challenge for all learners, and even the youngest students can begin to engage in this important aspect of mathematics learning.

The teacher has an important role in extending students' ideas. By asking questions or by reflecting on what a student has said, you engage not only that student but the rest of the class in thinking about an answer or statement. For example, in the activity Mystery Photos, students guess the location of numbers in photographs. By following up a student's response with "What clue in this picture makes you think this is a clock?" the student is encouraged to clarify his or her thinking. Posing a question to the whole class such as, "Who has a different idea?" extends the discussion and encourages the sharing of other ideas.

In Enough for the Class? (Investigation 4, Session 1), students share strategies for comparing two numbers. After a strategy is shared, a question such as, "Who used a strategy similar to Olga's?" encourages students to think about how their ideas are similar or different. "What different strategies did you use?" again extends the discussion and encourages a variety of responses.

Often asking "Why do you think that?" or "How do you know?" evokes the response "I just knew it" or no response at all. Sometimes reflecting back to a student, "I noticed that you made two towers of cubes when you were solving this problem" helps focus a student on his or her own process.

Reflecting on one's own thinking and considering the ideas of others evolves over time. Although young students are often egocentric in their approach to learning, they can begin to understand that an important part of doing mathematics is being able to explain your ideas and give reasons for your answers.

▪ D I A L O G U E ☐ B O X ▪

Patterns in Addition

During the activity Today's Number (p. 40), this class focuses on the number 10. The students draw from their experiences with the games Tens Go Fish and Turn Over 10 as they find combinations for 10.

The teacher focuses the group on looking at combinations of 10 using two addends. Students are asked how they can be sure they have found all the combinations, which sets the stage for possibly discovering an important number pattern. The following number sentences are listed on chart paper:

	10	
5 + 5	10 + 0	22 − 12
30 − 20	18 − 8	9 + 1
7 + 3	1 + 9	15 − 5
10 + 10 − 10		
4 + 3 + 2 + 1		
2 + 2 + 2 + 2 + 2		

You've found different ways to make 10. Let's look at just the number sentences that add two numbers, for example 5 + 5. Do you see or know any others? [*Teacher begins to make a separate list of these combinations.*]

Ayaz: There's 10 + 0 and 9 + 1 and 7 + 3. Those are on our list already.

Laura: There's 1 + 9, too.

Rosie: Isn't that a repeat, the same as 9 + 1?

Ayaz: Well, yes and no, I think. I think you should write it next to 9 + 1.

We talked about similar combinations the other day when we were finding ways to make 8. Some students thought they were the same and others thought they were different. Ayaz, your idea of writing them next to each other is a good one. OK, are there any others?

Harris: 6 + 4 makes 10 and so does 4 + 6.

Karina: You can also add 0 + 10.

So, do you think we have found all the combinations of two numbers that make 10? How could we be sure that we have them all?

Camilla: I think I see something about the numbers. It goes down from 10 then 9 then 7 and 6.

Ebony: I think there's something missing because it's like a pattern, but you need an 8 in there between the 9 and the 7. It would be 8 + 2.

[*The teacher writes 8 + 2 under 9 + 1.*]

Tim: And you need 2 + 8, too, on the other side.

Camilla: Now see the pattern I meant? The numbers on one side go down and on the other side go up. See, it's like if you had some cubes [*she takes 10 cubes from the bin on her table*] and you made two groups. Like 9 over here and then 1. Then if you make a group of 8, this one is less, but this group is more because it goes from 1 to 2.

Salim: And if you put the 5 + 5 under the 6 + 4, then that's sort of where the pattern turns and goes the other way. So I think we have them all.

So some of you are seeing a pattern with these combinations of 10. How many people think that we have found them all? How many aren't sure? I'm going to leave this chart here for a couple of days, and I'd like you to keep thinking about the pattern that Camilla and Salim noticed. If you discover another combination of 10 using two numbers, let us know and we'll add it to the list.

10 + 0	0 + 10
9 + 1	1 + 9
8 + 2	2 + 8
7 + 3	3 + 7
6 + 4	4 + 6
5 + 5	

The *Investigations* curriculum incorporates the use of two forms of technology in the classroom: calculators and computers. Calculators are assumed to be standard classroom materials, available for student use in any unit. Computers are explicitly linked to one or more units at each grade level; they are used with the unit on 2-D geometry at each grade, as well as with some of the units on measuring, data, and changes.

Using Calculators

In this curriculum, calculators are considered tools for doing mathematics, similar to pattern blocks or interlocking cubes. Just as with other tools, students must learn both *how* to use calculators correctly and *when* they are appropriate to use. This knowledge is crucial for daily life, as calculators are now a standard way of handling numerical operations, both at work and at home.

Using a calculator correctly is not a simple task; it depends on a good knowledge of the four operations and of the number system, so that students can select suitable calculations and also determine what a reasonable result would be. These skills are the basis of any work with numbers, whether or not a calculator is involved.

Unfortunately, calculators are often seen as tools to check computations with, as if other methods are somehow more fallible. Students need to understand that any computational method can be used to check any other; it's just as easy to make a mistake on the calculator as it is to make a mistake on paper or with mental arithmetic. Throughout this curriculum, we encourage students to solve computation problems in more than one way in order to double-check their accuracy. We present mental arithmetic, paper-and-pencil computation, and calculators as three possible approaches.

In this curriculum we also recognize that, despite their importance, calculators are not always appropriate in mathematics instruction. Like any tools, calculators are useful for some tasks but not for others. You will need to make decisions about when to allow students access to calculators and when to ask that they solve problems without them so that they can concentrate on other tools and skills. At times when calculators are or are not appropriate for a particular activity, we make specific recommendations. Help your students develop their own sense of which problems they can tackle with their own reasoning and which ones might be better solved with a combination of their own reasoning and the calculator.

Managing calculators in your classroom so that they are a tool, and not a distraction, requires some planning. When calculators are first introduced, students often want to use them for everything, even problems that can be solved quite simply by other methods. However, once the novelty wears off, students are just as interested in developing their own strategies, especially when these strategies are emphasized and valued in the classroom. Over time, students will come to recognize the ease and value of solving problems mentally, with paper and pencil, or with manipulatives, while also understanding the power of the calculator to facilitate work with larger numbers.

Experience shows that if calculators are available only occasionally, students become excited and distracted when they are permitted to use them. They focus on the tool rather than on the mathematics. In order to learn when calculators are appropriate and when they are not, students must have easy access to them and use them routinely in their work.

If you have a calculator for each student, and if you think your students can accept the responsibility, you might allow them to keep their calculators with the rest of their individual materials, at least for the first few weeks of school. Alternatively, you might store them in boxes on a shelf, number each calculator, and assign a corresponding number to each student. This system can give students a sense of ownership while also helping you keep track of the calculators.

Using Computers

Students can use computers to approach and visualize mathematical situations in new ways. The computer allows students to construct and manipulate geometric shapes, see objects move according to rules they specify, and turn, flip, and repeat a pattern.

This curriculum calls for computers in units where they are a particularly effective tool for learning mathematics content. One unit on 2-D geometry at each of the grades 3–5 includes a core of activities that rely on access to computers, either in the classroom or in a lab. Other units on geometry, measuring, data, and changes include computer activities, but can be taught without them. In these units, however, students' experience is greatly enhanced by computer use.

The following list outlines the recommended use of computers in this curriculum:

Kindergarten
Unit: *Making Shapes and Building Blocks* (Exploring Geometry)
Software: *Shapes*
Source: provided with the unit

Grade 1
Unit: *Survey Questions and Secret Rules* (Collecting and Sorting Data)
Software: *Tabletop, Jr.*
Source: Broderbund

Unit: *Quilt Squares and Block Towns* (2-D and 3-D Geometry)
Software: *Shapes*
Source: provided with the unit

Grade 2
Unit: *Mathematical Thinking at Grade 2* (Introduction)
Software: *Shapes*
Source: provided with the unit

Unit: *Shapes, Halves, and Symmetry* (Geometry and Fractions)
Software: *Shapes*
Source: provided with the unit

Unit: *How Long? How Far?* (Measuring)
Software: *Geo-Logo*
Source: provided with the unit

Grade 3
Unit: *Flips, Turns, and Area* (2-D Geometry)
Software: *Tumbling Tetrominoes*
Source: provided with the unit

Unit: *Turtle Paths* (2-D Geometry)
Software: *Geo-Logo*
Source: provided with the unit

Grade 4
Unit: *Sunken Ships and Grid Patterns* (2-D Geometry)
Software: *Geo-Logo*
Source: provided with the unit

Grade 5
Unit: *Picturing Polygons* (2-D Geometry)
Software: *Geo-Logo*
Source: provided with the unit

Unit: *Patterns of Change* (Tables and Graphs)
Software: *Trips*
Source: provided with the unit

Unit: *Data: Kids, Cats, and Ads* (Statistics)
Software: *Tabletop, Sr.*
Source: Broderbund

The software provided with the *Investigations* units uses the power of the computer to help students explore mathematical ideas and relationships that cannot be explored in the same way with physical materials. With the *Shapes* (grades 1–2) and *Tumbling Tetrominoes* (grade 3) software, students explore symmetry, pattern, rotation and reflection, area, and characteristics of 2-D shapes. With the *Geo-Logo* software (grades 2–5), students investigate rotations and reflections, coordinate geometry, the properties of 2-D shapes, and angles. The *Trips* software (grade 5) is a mathematical exploration of motion in which students run experiments and interpret data presented in graphs and tables.

We suggest that students work in pairs on the computer; this not only maximizes computer resources but also encourages students to consult, monitor, and teach each other. Generally, more than two students at one computer find it difficult to share. Managing access to computers is an issue for every classroom. The curriculum gives you explicit support for setting up a system. The units are structured on the assumption that you have enough computers for half your students to work on the machines in pairs at one time. If you do not have access to that many computers, suggestions are made for structuring class time to use the unit with fewer than five.

Assessment plays a critical role in teaching and learning, and it is an integral part of the *Investigations* curriculum. For a teacher using these units, assessment is an ongoing process. You observe students' discussions and explanations of their strategies on a daily basis and examine their work as it evolves. While students are busy recording and representing their work, working on projects, sharing with partners, and playing mathematical games, you have many opportunities to observe their mathematical thinking. What you learn through observation guides your decisions about how to proceed. In any of the units, you will repeatedly consider questions like these:

- Do students come up with their own strategies for solving problems, or do they expect others to tell them what to do? What do their strategies reveal about their mathematical understanding?

- Do students understand that there are different strategies for solving problems? Do they articulate their strategies and try to understand other students' strategies?

- How effectively do students use materials as tools to help with their mathematical work?

- Do students have effective ideas for keeping track of and recording their work? Do keeping track of and recording their work seem difficult for them?

You will need to develop a comfortable and efficient system for recording and keeping track of your observations. Some teachers keep a clipboard handy and jot notes on a class list or on adhesive labels that are later transferred to student files. Others keep loose-leaf notebooks with a page for each student and make weekly notes about what they have observed in class.

Assessment Tools in the Unit

With the activities in each unit, you will find questions to guide your thinking while observing the students at work. You will also find two built-in assessment tools: Teacher Checkpoints and embedded Assessment activities.

Teacher Checkpoints The designated Teacher Checkpoints in each unit offer a time to "check in" with individual students, watch them at work, and ask questions that illuminate how they are thinking.

At first it may be hard to know what to look for, hard to know what kinds of questions to ask. Students may be reluctant to talk; they may not be accustomed to having the teacher ask them about their work, or they may not know how to explain their thinking. Two important ingredients of this process are asking students open-ended questions about their work and showing genuine interest in how they are approaching the task. When students see that you are interested in their thinking and are counting on them to come up with their own ways of solving problems, they may surprise you with the depth of their understanding.

Teacher Checkpoints also give you the chance to pause in the teaching sequence and reflect on how your class is doing overall. Think about whether you need to adjust your pacing: Are most students fluent with strategies for solving a particular kind of problem? Are they just starting to formulate good strategies? Or are they still struggling with how to start? Depending on what you see as the students work, you may want to spend more time on similar problems, change some of the problems to use smaller numbers, move quickly to more challenging material, modify subsequent activities for some students, work on particular ideas with a small group, or pair students who have good strategies with those who are having more difficulty.

Embedded Assessment Activities Assessment activities embedded in each unit will help you examine specific pieces of student work, figure out what they mean, and provide feedback. From the students' point of view, these assessment activities are no different from any others. Each is a learning experience in and of itself, as well as an opportunity for you to gather evidence about students' mathematical understanding.

The embedded assessment activities sometimes involve writing and reflecting; at other times, a discussion or brief interaction between student and teacher; and in still other instances, the creation and explanation of a product. In most cases, the assessments require that students *show* what they did, *write* or *talk* about it, or do both. Having to explain how they worked through a problem helps students be more focused and clear in their mathematical thinking. It also helps them realize that doing mathematics is a process that may involve tentative starts, revising one's approach, taking different paths, and working through ideas.

Teachers often find the hardest part of assessment to be interpreting their students' work. We provide guidelines to help with that interpretation. If you have used a process approach to teaching writing, the assessment in *Investigations* will seem familiar. For many of the assessment activities, a Teacher Note provides examples of student work and a commentary on what it indicates about student thinking.

Documentation of Student Growth

To form an overall picture of mathematical progress, it is important to document each student's work. Many teachers have students keep their work in folders, notebooks, or journals, and some like to have students summarize their learning in journals at the end of each unit. It's important to document students' progress, and we recommend that you keep a portfolio of selected work for each student, unit by unit, for the entire year. The final activity in each *Investigations* unit, called Choosing Student Work to Save, helps you and the students select representative samples for a record of their work.

This kind of regular documentation helps you synthesize information about each student as a mathematical learner. From different pieces of evidence, you can put together the big picture. This synthesis will be invaluable in thinking about where to go next with a particular child, deciding where more work is needed, or explaining to parents (or other teachers) how a child is doing.

If you use portfolios, you need to collect a good balance of work, yet avoid being swamped with an overwhelming amount of paper. Following are some tips for effective portfolios:

- Collect a representative sample of work, including some pieces that students themselves select for inclusion in the portfolio. There should be just a few pieces for each unit, showing different kinds of work—some assignments that involve writing as well as some that do not.

- If students do not date their work, do so yourself so that you can reconstruct the order in which pieces were done.

- Include your reflections on the work. When you are looking back over the whole year, such comments are reminders of what seemed especially interesting about a particular piece; they can also be helpful to other teachers and to parents. Older students should be encouraged to write their own reflections about their work.

Assessment Overview

There are two places to turn for a preview of the assessment opportunities in each *Investigations* unit. The Assessment Resources column in the unit Overview Chart identifies the Teacher Checkpoints and Assessment activities embedded in each investigation, guidelines for observing the students that appear within classroom activities, and any Teacher Notes and Dialogue Boxes that explain what to look for and what types of student responses you might expect to see in your classroom. Additionally, the section About the Assessment in This Unit gives you a detailed list of questions for each investigation, keyed to the mathematical emphases, to help you observe student growth.

Depending on your situation, you may want to provide additional assessment opportunities. Most of the investigations lend themselves to more frequent assessment, simply by having students do more writing and recording while they are working.

Mathematical Thinking at Grade 2

Content of the Unit This unit introduces second graders to some of the content, processes, and materials they will be using to solve problems in mathematics. As the year begins, students explore counting and categorization in each of the three areas of the *Investigations* curriculum: number, data, and space (geometry). They also are introduced to two of the three mathematical routines (Today's Number and How Many Pockets?) that will be part of their classroom throughout the year.

Throughout the unit, students work with some of the mathematical tools and materials (interlocking cubes, pattern blocks, coins, and Geoblocks) they will be using all year. They are also engaged in critical mathematical processes such as solving problems and sharing strategies, writing and drawing about their work, working with peers, and using materials.

Students are also introduced to *Shapes*, one of two software programs that were developed especially for the curriculum. *Shapes* is introduced in this unit and used during the Geometry and Fractions unit. Although the *Shapes* software is specially included in only these units, we recommend that students use it throughout the year. The computer activities are very motivational to students. As the activities can be done again and again, students develop skills and insights as they use the software.

This unit is designed to help you get to know and assess students' mathematical understanding; it is also designed to help you establish a mathematical community and environment. The unit offers suggestions and ideas of ways to organize the environment and materials and ways to establish classroom routines.

Connections with Other Units If you are doing the full-year *Investigations* curriculum in the suggested sequence for grade 2, this is the first of eight units. It has connections with every other unit in the second grade sequence, both in its content and in its emphasis on ways of thinking and doing mathematics.

If your school is not using the full-year curriculum, this unit can successfully be used at any time of the year as a way to help students focus on thinking, working, and talking mathematically, as well as to assess student understanding of some key mathematical content at this grade level.

Investigations Curriculum ■ Suggested Grade 2 Sequence

▶ *Mathematical Thinking at Grade 2* (Introduction)

Coins, Coupons, and Combinations (The Number System)

Does It Walk, Crawl, or Swim? (Sorting and Classifying Data)

Shapes, Halves, and Symmetry (Geometry and Fractions)

Putting Together and Taking Apart (Addition and Subtraction)

How Long? How Far? (Measuring)

How Many Pockets? How Many Teeth? (Collecting and Representing Data)

Timelines and Rhythm Patterns (Representing Time)

Investigation 1 ▪ Exploring Materials

Class Sessions	Activities	Pacing
Session 1 (p. 4) EXPLORING CUBES AND ARRANGEMENTS OF 10	Exploring Interlocking Cubes 10 Cubes Introducing Math Folders and Weekly Logs Homework: Arranging 10 Objects	minimum 1 hr
Sessions 2 and 3 (p. 10) EXPLORING CUBES, PATTERN BLOCKS, AND GEOBLOCKS	Exploring Pattern Blocks and Geoblocks Class Discussion: What Did You Discover? Weekly Logs Homework: What Is Mathematics?	minimum 2 hr
Session 4 (p. 15) BUILDING AND SORTING CUBE THINGS	Building Cube Things Sorting Cube Things	minimum 1 hr

Mathematical Emphasis

- Exploring materials used in this unit and throughout the curriculum

- Describing and sorting materials on the basis of their attributes

- Identifying categories for different things

- Counting a set of objects

- Writing number expressions to describe configurations of cubes

Assessment Resources

Exploring Pattern Blocks and Geoblocks: Observing the Students (p. 11)

Exploring Materials (Dialogue Box, p. 14)

Sorting Cube Things (Dialogue Box, p. 18)

Materials

Interlocking cubes

Tubs or shoe boxes

Student math folders

Pattern blocks

Geoblocks

Index cards or paper

Plain paper

Student Sheets 1–3

Family letter

Investigation 2 ■ Looking at Numbers

Class Sessions	Activities	Pacing
Session 1 (p. 22) HOW MANY DAYS HAVE WE BEEN IN SCHOOL?	Today's Number: Ways to Make 5 Uses of Numbers Homework: How Do You Use Numbers?	minimum 1 hr
Sessions 2 and 3 (p. 26) CARD GAMES	Tens Go Fish Turn Over 10 Introducing Choice Time Homework: Playing Card Games at Home	minimum 2 hr
Sessions 4 and 5 (p. 35) MYSTERY PHOTOS	Mystery Photos Building Cube Things Choice Time Homework: More Card Games at Home	minimum 2 hr
Session 6 (p. 40) TODAY'S NUMBER AND COUNTING POCKETS	Today's Number How Many Pockets? Writing About Pockets Homework: Pockets at Home	minimum 1 hr
Session 7 (p. 46) REVEALING MYSTERY PHOTOS	Choice Time Revealing Mystery Photos	minimum 1 hr
Session 8 (p. 49) WAYS TO GET TO 12	Ways to Get to 11 Teacher Checkpoint: Ways to Get to 12 Homework: Ways to Get to _____	minimum 1 hr

Start-Up ■ Today's Number, Uses of Numbers, Playing Number Games at Home, Pockets at Home

---

Mathematical Emphasis

- Keeping track of the number of school days

- Writing equations that equal the number of days in school

- Making combinations of 10

- Identifying uses of number in the world

Assessment Resources

Introducing Choice Time: Observing the Students (p. 30)

Keeping Track of Students' Work (Teacher Note, p. 34)

Choice Time: Observing the Students (p. 38)

Patterns in Addition (Dialogue Box, p. 45)

Teacher Checkpoint: Ways to Get to 12 (p. 50)

Materials

Index cards

Adding-machine tape

Interlocking cubes

Resealable plastic bags or envelopes

Chart paper or newsprint

Overhead projector

Large jar

Masking or colored tape or rubber band

12 Ways to Get to 11 by Eve Merriam (opt.)

Student Sheets 4–10

Teaching resource sheets

Investigation 3 ■ Geometric Counts

Class Sessions	Activities	Pacing
Sessions 1 and 2 (p. 54) GEOBLOCK FACES AND PATTERN BLOCK PUZZLES	On-Computer Activity: Introducing *Shapes* Software Find the Block Ways to Fill Choice Time Homework: More Card Games at Home Extension: Pattern Block Designs	minimum 2 hr
Sessions 3 and 4 (p. 64) COUNTING GEOBLOCKS AND PATTERN BLOCKS	How Many Different Geoblocks? Cover and Count Choice Time Homework: Tomorrow's Number	minimum 2 hr
Session 5 (p. 68) SORTING GEOBLOCKS	Teacher Checkpoint: Sorting Geoblocks Choice Time	minimum 1 hr
Session 6 (p. 72) PATTERN BLOCK COUNTS	Cover and Count: How Many Blocks? On-Computer Activity: Solve *Shapes* Puzzles Opening the Geoblock Count Box Homework: Finding Shapes	minimum 1 hr

Start-Up ■ Today's Number

Mathematical Emphasis

- Exploring and describing two-dimensional geometric shapes

- Exploring, sorting, and describing three-dimensional geometric shapes

- Finding different shapes and arrangements to cover patterns

- Finding and recording several solutions to a problem

Assessment Resources

Choice Time: Observing the Students (p. 59)

Choice Time: Observing the Students (p. 66)

Teacher Checkpoint: Sorting Geoblocks (p. 68)

Choice Time: Observing the Students (p. 71)

On-Computer Activity: Solve *Shapes* Puzzles: Observing the Students (p. 74)

Materials

Pattern blocks

Geoblocks

Overhead projector

Resealable plastic bags or envelopes

Paper or cloth bags

Index cards

Stick-on notes

Computers

Shapes (Apple Macintosh disk)

Projection device or large-screen monitor

Paper (12" by 18" and 8 1/2" by 11")

Student Sheets 11–18

Teaching resource sheets

Investigation 4 ■ Counting

Class Sessions	Activities	Pacing
Session 1 (p. 78) ENOUGH FOR THE CLASS?	How Many People Are in Our Class? Enough for the Class?	minimum 1 hr
Session 2 (p. 86) COUNTING COINS, COUNTING CHOICES	Exploring Coins Collect 25¢ Choice Time Homework: Exploring Coins Extension: Number Cubes	minimum 1 hr
Sessions 3 and 4 (p. 92) COUNTING STRIPS AND COUNTING CHOICES	Counting Strips Choice Time Class Discussion: Counting Strips Homework: Counting Strips	minimum 2 hr
Session 5 (p. 96) ENOUGH FOR THE CLASS? REVISITED	Assessment: Enough for the Class?	minimum 1 hr

Start-Up ■ Today's Number

Mathematical Emphasis

- Counting 15–60 objects
- Counting by 2's, 5's, 10's, and other ways
- Comparing two sets by identifying how many more are needed or how many are extra
- Adding two-digit numbers
- Identifying coins and their values
- Combining coins to make 25¢ and 50¢

Assessment Resources

Writing and Recording (Teacher Note, p. 82)

Are There Enough for the Class? (Dialogue Box, p. 85)

Choice Time: Observing the Students (p. 89)

Observing Students Counting (Teacher Note, p. 91)

Choice Time: Observing the Students (p. 93)

Assessment: Enough for the Class? (p. 96)

Assessment: Enough for the Class? (Teacher Note, p. 98)

Materials

Interlocking cubes

Resealable plastic bags or envelopes

Countable objects

Chart paper

Plastic coin sets or real coins

Small cups

Number cubes

Tape

Adding-machine tape

Student Sheets 19–21

Investigation 5 ▪ Collecting Data About Ourselves

Class Sessions	Activities	
Sessions 1 and 2 (p. 102) COLLECTING AND REPRESENTING DATA ABOUT OURSELVES	Playing Guess My Rule Collecting and Recording Guess My Rule Data Representing Guess My Rule Data Representing Data with Categories Homework: Tomorrow's Number Using Three Numbers	minimum 2 hr
Session 3 (p. 113) COLLECTING POCKET DATA	How Many Pockets? Teacher Checkpoint: Today's Number Homework: How Many Pockets?	minimum 1 hr
Sessions 4 and 5 (p. 116) TAKING INVENTORIES	What Can We Count? Taking a Classroom Inventory Class Discussion: How Did You Count? Homework: Inventory Extension: People Inventory	minimum 2 hr
Session 6 (p. 122) REPRESENTING INVENTORY DATA	Assessment: Representing Home Inventories Choosing Student Work to Save	minimum 1 hr

Start-Up ▪ **Today's Number**

Mathematical Emphasis

- Sorting and classifying information

- Collecting, recording, and representing data

- Counting and comparing amounts

- Counting groups of objects in more than one way

- Talking and writing about problem-solving strategies

Assessment Resources

Representing Guess My Rule Data: Observing the Students (p. 106)

Inventing Pictures of the Data (Teacher Note, p. 111)

Playing Guess My Rule (Dialogue Box, p. 112)

Teacher Checkpoint: Today's Number (p. 115)

Taking a Classroom Inventory: Observing the Students (p. 118)

Choosing Things to Inventory (Dialogue Box, p. 121)

Assessment: Representing Home Inventories (p. 122)

Choosing Student Work to Save (p. 123)

Materials

Paper (plain, 8 1/2" by 11")

Chart paper

Interlocking cubes

Markers or crayons

Large jar

Masking or colored tape or rubber band

Large paper (12" by 18")

Student Sheets 22–24

Following are the basic materials needed for the activities in this unit. Many of the items can be purchased from the publisher, either individually or in the Teacher Resource Package and the Student Materials Kit for grade 2. Detailed information is available on the *Investigations* order form. To obtain this form, call toll-free 1-800-872-1100 and ask for a Dale Seymour customer service representative.

Geoblocks: l or 2 sets, each divided into 2–3 subsets

Snap™ Cubes (interlocking cubes): about 30 per student

Pattern blocks: 1 bucket per 6–8 students

Standard dot or number cubes with numbers or dots 1–6: l per group of 3–4 students

Primary Number Cards, referred to as Number Cards throughout the unit (manufactured; or use blackline masters to make your own sets): 1 set per student

Plastic coin sets (real coins may be substituted), 30 pennies, 20 nickels, 20 dimes: 1 set per 3–4 students

Containers for coin sets: 1 per set

Computers: Macintosh II or above, with 4 MB of internal memory (RAM) and Apple System Software 7.0 or later. Maximum, 1 for every 2 students. Minimum, 1 for every 4–6 students.

Apple Macintosh disk, *Shapes–Mathematical Thinking* (packaged with this book)

A projection device or large-screen monitor on one computer for whole-class viewing (optional)

Adding-machine tape

Index cards

Stick-on notes

Chart paper or newsprint

Folders for student work: 1 per student

Resealable plastic bags or envelopes

Tape

Markers, crayons

Large jar

Masking or colored tape, or a rubber band that fits the jar

Overhead projector (optional)

Paper—plain 8½" by 11" and 12" by 18"

Paper or cloth bags: 3 or 4

12 Ways to Get to 11 by Eve Merriam (optional)

The following materials are provided at the end of this unit as blackline masters. A Student Activity Booklet containing all student sheets and teaching resources needed for individual work is available.

Family Letter (p. 174)

Student Sheets 1–24 (p. 175)

Teaching Resources:

    100 Chart (p. 185)

    Number Cards (p. 186)

    Mystery Photo Cards (p. 190)

    Find the Block Task Cards (p. 202)

Practice Pages (p. 215)

Related Children's Literature

Adams, Barbara. *The Go-Round Dollar.* New York: Four Winds Press, 1992.

Artitage, Ronda and David. *Grandma Goes Shopping.* New York: Puffin, 1995.

Holtzman, Caren. *A Quarter from the Tooth Fairy.* New York: Scholastic, 1995.

Merriam, Eve. *12 Ways to Get to 11.* New York: Simon and Schuster, 1993.

Payne, Emmy. *Katy No-Pocket.* Boston: Houghton Mifflin, 1972.

Rice, Eve. *Peter's Pockets.* New York: Greenwillow Books, 1989.

Thornhill, Jan. *The Wildlife 1•2•3.* New York: Simon and Schuster, 1989.

Winthrop, Elizabeth. *Shoes.* New York: Harper and Row, 1986.

Mathematical Thinking at Grade 2, as the title indicates, is designed to be an introduction to mathematical thinking—to some of the content, materials, processes, and ways of working that mathematics entails. The investigations in this unit engage students in:

- solving mathematical problems in ways that make sense to them
- talking, writing, and drawing about their work
- working with peers
- exploring materials and using them to build models of mathematical situations
- relying on their own thinking
- learning from the thinking of others

Students work with counting and classifying in each of the three areas of the *Investigations* curriculum, of number, data, and space (geometry). In number, they count objects in various ways, write number sentences and expressions to represent numbers, combine and compare two quantities, and work on addition combinations, especially combinations for 10. Their work with geometry includes sorting and describing two- and three-dimensional shapes, exploring how different shapes can be put together to make other shapes, and finding equivalent ways to cover a pattern or build a block. This work is done with two- and three-dimensional blocks. In addition, students explore these ideas using a computer software program called *Shapes*. In the data investigation, students continue their work with counting and classifying when they collect, sort, and represent data about themselves and things they inventory in the classroom and at home.

A major focus of these activities is the development and use of good number sense to count, combine, and compare one-digit and two-digit numbers. Just as common sense grows from experience with the world and how it works, number sense grows from experience with how numbers work. While almost all students entering second grade can fluently count small quantities, they vary tremendously in their ability to count larger amounts and to represent any amount in a variety of ways. Students are encouraged to build upon what they do know in ways that are challenging but not threatening. For

example, in two card games, students work on combinations of 10. Some students will need to use objects to figure out what number matches a particular card, while others will become quite facile in recalling all the combinations.

Mathematical Thinking at Grade 2 is designed not only to involve students with some central mathematical concepts, but also to introduce students to a particular way of approaching mathematics. Throughout the unit students are encouraged to share their strategies, work cooperatively, use materials, and communicate both verbally and in writing about how they are solving problems. These approaches may be quite difficult for some students. Even taking out, using, and putting away materials may be unfamiliar. Certainly writing and drawing pictures to describe mathematical thinking will be quite difficult for some students. This unit is a time to focus on the development of these processes: to spend time establishing routines and expectations, to communicate to students your own interest in and respect for their mathematical ideas, to assure students that you want to know about their *thinking* and not just their answers, and to insist that students work hard to solve problems in ways that make sense to them. As the unit unfolds, a mathematical community begins to take shape—a community that you and your students are together responsible for creating and maintaining.

At the beginning of each investigation, the Mathematical Emphasis section tells you what is most important for students to learn about during that investigation. Many of these mathematical understandings and processes are difficult and complex. Students gradually learn more and more about each idea over many years of schooling. Individual students will begin and end the unit with different levels of knowledge and skill, but all will gain greater knowledge about solving mathematical problems in number, data, and space (geometry), in ways that make sense to them.

Throughout the *Investigations* curriculum, there are many opportunities for ongoing daily assessment as you observe, listen to, and interact with students at work. In this unit, you will find three Teacher Checkpoints:

Investigation 2, Session 8:
Ways to Get to 12 (p. 50)

Investigation 3, Session 5:
Sorting Geoblocks (p. 68)

Investigation 5, Session 3:
Today's Number (p. 115)

This unit also has two embedded assessment activities:

Investigation 4, Session 5:
Enough for the Class? (p. 96)

Investigation 5, Session 6:
Representing Home Inventories (p. 122)

In addition, you can use almost any activity in this unit to assess your students' needs and strengths. Listed below are questions to help you focus your observations in each investigation. You may want to keep track of your observations for each student to help you plan your curriculum and monitor students' growth. Suggestions for documenting student growth can be found in the section About Assessment.

Investigation 1: Exploring Materials

■ What do students notice about the materials? Are students already familiar with any of them? What do they do with the materials? Do they seem engaged as they explore? Do they initiate their own ideas, observe others, or follow given prompts or suggestions? Are there patterns or symmetry in what they make?

■ How do students describe the materials? Are students able to identify attributes of a material and group objects with like attributes?

■ How do students describe the categories for their groups as they sort? What attributes of objects do students attend to? Are they able to ignore certain characteristics in order to focus on other attributes of the same object?

■ How do students count a set of 30 objects? Can they count by 1's and by 2's or 5's? Do they count accurately?

■ How do students write number expressions to describe configurations of cubes? Do they account for each cube once and only once? Do their number expressions match their cube configurations?

Investigation 2: Looking at Numbers

■ What kinds of equations do students write to equal the number of school days? Do they check their own and others' equations? Are they able to generate more than one combination of numbers to equal a given total? Do they see patterns in the equations? Do they have favorite kinds of number sentences? Do students use materials in order to generate ways to make a number?

■ How familiar are students with number combinations of 10? Do they use materials to figure the combinations out? Do they count-on to 10 from one number? Are they able to predict how much more they need to make a total of 10? Do they use combinations they know to help them figure out new combinations? Do they see patterns in the combinations?

■ How familiar are students with the ways numbers are used in the world? How broad is their awareness? Can they identify how numbers are used as well as places where they can be found?

Investigation 3: Geometric Counts

■ How do students describe two-dimensional shapes? What attributes do they identify? What kinds of relationships do they see among shapes? Can they identify common attributes of different shapes?

■ How do students describe three-dimensional shapes? What words do they use to describe the shapes' attributes? What kinds of relationships do they see among the shapes? How do they sort the shapes?

■ How do students cover shapes with pattern blocks? Do they place blocks in a systematic way? Do they predict what blocks will fit into spaces? Do they realize that they can replace some shapes with combinations of other shapes (for example, replacing a hexagon with 2 trapezoids)?

How comfortable are students in finding more than one solution to a problem? For example, do they use relationships between the blocks when covering a shape a second or third time? Do they clear the blocks off the shape and then begin placing blocks again randomly?

Investigation 4: Counting

■ How do students count a group of objects? Do they count by 1's? by other groups like 2's or 5's? Do they touch or move each object? How do they keep track of the objects they've counted? Do they count each object once and only once? If children group the objects by some number, do they count by that number or by 1's? Do students realize that counting by 1's and counting by a group will give them the same quantity? Do they double-check their count?

■ How do students compare the quantities of two sets of objects? How familiar are they with language such as more than/less than? What strategies do they use to compare two quantities? What materials do students use?

■ How do students add two-digit numbers? Do they count-on from one of the numbers? Do they solve the problem by breaking the two numbers apart into meaningful "chunks" and then recombining them? What materials do students use?

■ How familiar are students with coins and their values?

■ How do students combine coins to make 25 cents or 50 cents? Are students able to count out their coins accurately? Do students collect their coins in pennies? Do they know and use coin equivalencies? Do they trade coins for coins of equal value?

Investigation 5: Collecting Data About Ourselves

■ How do students sort and classify information? What characteristics do students attend to as they sort and classify?

■ How do students collect, record, and represent data? Do students imitate others' representations of data or create new ways? Do students keep track of and account for all the pieces of data? How? When recording data, what materials do students use?

■ How do students count and compa[re]... What materials do students use? Do students count the difference between the two sets? Do they directly compare two sets of objects or do they rely on mental manipulations of the quantities?

■ Do students count the same group of objects in more than one way? Are students aware that the same group of objects should have the same quantity in it no matter how it is counted? How do they organize the task and keep track of their count? How do they record the information they collect?

■ How comfortable are students with talking and writing about mathematical strategies? How clearly can they articulate their ideas orally and in writing? Do they listen and respond to others' strategies?

Thinking and Working in Mathematics

This unit provides the chance for you to observe students' work habits and communication skills. Think about these questions to help you decide which routines, processes, and materials will require the most support.

■ How comfortable are students in various types of work situations? Are they able to work alone? with a partner? How they participate in whole-group discussions?

■ How do students respond to Choice Time sessions? Are they self-directed and able to make choices independently? Do students move comfortably between activities, or do they stick with a familiar and safe choice? Do students complete each activity, or do they move around quickly from activity to activity?

■ How do students interact with peers? Do they share ideas? share materials? work cooperatively? Or do they prefer to work independently?

■ Do students have ideas about how to record their work with words, numbers, or pictures?

■ What types of materials or activities do individual students seem most (or least) comfortable with?

In the *Investigations* curriculum, mathematical vocabulary is introduced naturally during the activities. We don't ask students to learn definitions of new terms; rather, they come to understand such words as *data, graph, area,* and *symmetry* by hearing them used frequently in discussion as they investigate new concepts. This approach is compatible with current theories of second-language acquisition, which emphasize the use of new vocabulary in meaningful contexts while students are actively involved with objects, pictures, and physical movement.

Listed below are some key words used in this unit that will not be new to most English speakers at this age level, but may be unfamiliar to students with limited English proficiency. You will want to spend additional time working on these words with your students who are learning English. If your students are working with a second-language teacher, you might enlist your colleague's aid in familiarizing students with these words before and during this unit. In the classroom, look for opportunities for students to hear and use these words. Activities you can use to present the words are given in the appendix, Vocabulary Support for Second-Language Learners (p. 133).

similar, same, different   Students use these terms as they compare the attributes of objects and of people.

more, fewer   These terms are used throughout the unit as students count and compare quantities, follow directions, and check answers.

Multicultural Extensions for All Students

Whenever possible, encourage students to share words, objects, customs, or any aspects of daily life from their own cultures and backgrounds that are relevant to the activities in this unit. For example:

■ As students count in Investigation 1, they may enjoy sharing words for numbers they know in other languages. Students may enjoy teaching these counting names to the others in the class.

■ Extend the counting and recording of school days by first discussing with students how many days are in the school year. Visit the library together and research the number of days children attend school in other countries.

■ As students count coins in Investigation 4, encourage them to bring in or tell about any foreign coins they have at home. Students might share the name of the coin, its value, and its country of origin.

■ As students record data about themselves in Investigation 5, encourage them to discuss and share any collection of multicultural objects they may have. Students may want to tell about the objects they have in these special collections, and how many objects they have.

Investigations

Exploring Materials

What Happens

Session 1: Exploring Cubes and Arrangements of 10 Students explore interlocking cubes and describe their characteristics. They make arrangements of 10 cubes and describe them using number sentences.

Sessions 2 and 3: Exploring Cubes, Pattern Blocks, and Geoblocks Students are introduced to pattern blocks and Geoblocks. These, in addition to the interlocking cubes, are used for free exploration. Students describe the characteristics of the three materials, noting similarities and differences.

Session 4: Building and Sorting Cube Things Students count out 30 cubes and use them to build a Cube Thing. They share their Cube Things and sort them in several ways.

Mathematical Emphasis

- Exploring materials used in this unit and throughout the curriculum
- Describing and sorting materials on the basis of their attributes
- Identifying categories for different things
- Counting a set of objects
- Writing number expressions to describe configurations of cubes

What to Plan Ahead of Time

Materials

- Interlocking cubes: at least 30 per student (Sessions 1–4)
- Tubs or shoe boxes for storing interlocking cubes (Sessions 1–4)
- Student math folders (made from oaktag or construction paper): 1 per student (Session 1)
- Plain paper: 1 sheet per student (Session 1)
- Pattern blocks: l bucket per 6–8 students (Sessions 2–3)
- Geoblocks: 1–2 sets per classroom (Sessions 2–3)
- Index cards or paper: 1 per student (Session 4)

Other Preparation

- Duplicate the following student sheets and teaching resources (located at the end of this unit) in the following quantities. If you have Student Activity Booklets, copy only the item marked with an asterisk.

  For Session 1

  Family letter* (p. 174): 1 per student. Remember to sign and date the letter before copying it.

  Student Sheet 1, Weekly Log (p. 175): 1 per student. At this time you may want to duplicate a supply to last for the entire unit and distribute the sheets as needed.

  Student Sheet 2, Arranging 10 Objects (p. 176): 1 per student (homework)

  For Sessions 2–3

  Student Sheet 3, What Is Mathematics? (p. 177): 1 per student (homework)

- Familiarize yourself with interlocking cubes, pattern blocks, and Geoblocks by doing students' tasks in this investigation. If you have not used the materials before, spend some time freely exploring them. (Session 1)

- Separate each set of Geoblocks into two or three equal sets. If divided into three sets, there will be enough blocks for two or three students to use together at one time. If divided into two sets, there will be enough for four or five students to use together. Probably the easiest way to divide the blocks is to find two (or three) identical blocks and put one in each set. If you have parent volunteers, aides, or older student volunteers, they can do this task. (Sessions 2–3)

- Prepare a math folder for each student. (Session 1)

Exploring Cubes and Arrangements of 10

Materials

- Interlocking cubes (at least 30 per student)
- Student math folders (1 per student)
- Student Sheet 1 (1 per student)
- Family letter (1 per student)
- Student Sheet 2 (1 per student, homework)
- Plain paper (1 sheet per student)

What Happens

Students explore interlocking cubes and describe their characteristics. They make arrangements of 10 cubes and describe them using number sentences. Their work focuses on:

- exploring interlocking cubes
- using number sentences to describe a configuration of 10 cubes
- keeping track of their daily work

Activity

Exploring Interlocking Cubes

Begin with a brief discussion about some of the tools students will be using and the kind of work they will be doing in this unit.

In our mathematics class this year, you will be using numbers in many different ways. You will also be using lots of different materials and tools to help you solve problems. We will use tools like cubes, calculators, and pattern blocks to solve math problems and play math games.

Ask students if they are familiar with any of these materials and how they have used them in the past. Then introduce interlocking cubes as one of the tools students will be using.

When introducing any new material, it is important to establish clear ground rules. You will want to discuss where cubes are stored and how they will be used and cared for. See the **Teacher Note**, Materials as Tools for Learning (p. 9), for hints about establishing routines for using and caring for manipulatives.

Often you will want students to stop working and to focus their attention on a discussion. Because materials may be out on tables, some students may be distracted and continue playing with them during the discussion. It is important to set clear limits during these first sessions.

Allow about 20 minutes for students to explore the cubes. At the end of this exploratory time, ask students to check the floor for cubes and return all cubes to their containers (or push them to the middle of the table). Many teachers have found that giving a warning a few minutes before the end of a work period helps students be aware that a transition is about to occur. Establishing such routines is emphasized throughout this introductory unit.

Discuss what students noticed about the cubes. They may mention characteristics such as the cubes are different colors, have knobs, and attach together. Ask questions such as:

- **What do you notice about the cubes?**
- **Pick up one cube, look at it closely, and tell me about it.**
- **How many different colors are there?**
- **What did you do with the cubes today?**
- **How do you think the cubes might be used during math class?**

Activity

10 Cubes

Each student takes 10 cubes, one cube of each color, and connects them to make an object or pattern that will stay connected when picked up.

Discuss the different arrangements of cubes.

Everyone has 10 cubes, one of each color. I made an arrangement that looks like a set of stairs. If I were going to describe this using numbers, I might say it's 4 + 3 + 2 + 1. How would you describe your arrangement of 10 cubes using numbers?

Students share their cube arrangements by describing them using numbers as they hold them up. Some possible arrangements are:

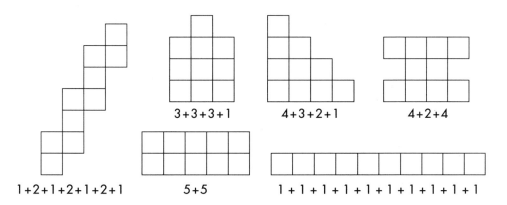

3 + 3 + 3 + 1   4 + 3 + 2 + 1   4 + 2 + 4

1 + 2 + 1 + 2 + 1 + 2 + 1   5 + 5   1 + 1 + 1 + 1 + 1 + 1 + 1 + 1 + 1 + 1

Record their numerical descriptions on the board as you acknowledge all the various ways to make 10.

Give each student a sheet of paper. Ask them to write "10 Cubes" at the top of their paper and then record their numerical descriptions. They can also try to draw their cube arrangement next to the number sentence.

Then students can make a new arrangement of 10 cubes. When most have finished, ask them to share their cube structure with partners or someone sitting nearby. Encourage them to describe their new arrangement by using numbers. Again, they should record this information on their 10 Cubes sheet. If there is time, students can continue to find different arrangements for 10 cubes.

<hr>

Activity

Introducing Math Folders and Weekly Logs

Before introducing students to their math folders, have them return all the cubes to the bins. Remind them to check the floor for stray cubes.

Near the end of this session, tell students about the way they will keep track of the math work they do this year.

Mathematicians show how they think about and solve problems by talking about their work, drawing pictures, building models, and explaining their work in writing so that they can share their ideas with other people. Your math folder will be a place to collect the writing and drawing that you do in math class.

Distribute a math folder to each student and have them label the folders with their name.

Your math folder is a place to keep track of what you do each day in math class. Sometimes you will choose more than one activity from several, and other times, like today, everyone will do the same thing. Each day you will record what you did on a weekly log.

Distribute Student Sheet 1, Weekly Log, and ask students to write their name at the top. Point out that there are spaces for each day of the week and ask them to write today's date on the line after the appropriate day. You may wish to have students include the month (spelled out), the day, and the year, or you may want them to use abbreviations (Sept. 9, 1996, or 9/9/96). Discuss what the box beside the date is for.

The box beside the date is for keeping track of how many days we have been in school this year. Since today is the first day of school [*adjust accordingly*], write a 1 in the box. What number will you write in the box tomorrow? What number will you write on Friday [*or name the next school day*]?

Print the titles of today's activities, "Exploring Cubes" and "10 Cubes," on the board and have students write them in the space below the date. Titles for choices and whole-class activities should be short to encourage all students to record what they do each day.

❖ **Tip for the Linguistically Diverse Classroom** Encourage students who are not writing comfortably in English to use drawings to record in their Weekly Log. If students demonstrate some proficiency in writing, suggest that they record a few words with their drawings.

Students can also record a sample problem, representative of each day's work.

Weekly Logs can be stapled to the front of the folders with each new week on the top, so students can view prior logs by lifting up the sheets.

During the unit (or throughout the year) you might use the math folders and Weekly Logs in a number of ways:

- to keep track of what kind of activities students choose to do and how frequently they choose them
- to review with students, individually or as a group, the work they've accomplished
- to share student work with families; either by sending folders home periodically for students to share or during student/family/teacher conferences

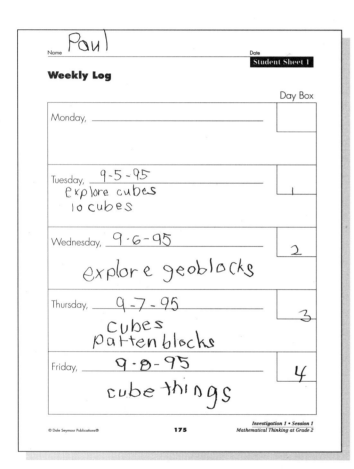

Session 1 Follow-Up

 **Homework**

Arranging 10 Objects Send home the family letter or the *Investigations at Home* booklet, as well as Student Sheet 2, Arranging 10 Objects. Students find 10 small objects at home and make several arrangements with them. They record at least two of their arrangements on the student sheet.

Materials as Tools for Learning

Concrete materials are used throughout the *Investigations* curriculum as tools for learning. Students of all ages benefit from being able to use materials to model problems and explain their thinking.

The more available materials are, the more likely students are to use them. Having materials available means that they are readily accessible to students and that students are allowed to make decisions about which tools to use and when to use them. In much the same way as you choose the best tool to use for certain projects or tasks, students should be encouraged to think about which material best meets their needs.

It is important to encourage all students to use materials. If manipulatives are used only when someone is having difficulty, students can get the mistaken idea that using materials is a less sophisticated and less valued way of solving a problem. Encourage students to talk about how they used certain materials. They should see how different people, including the teacher, use a variety of materials in solving the same problem.

Using concrete materials in the classroom may be a new experience for many students and teachers. Before introducing new materials, think about how you want students to use and care for them and how they will be stored.

Introducing a New Material Students need time to explore a new material before using it in structured activities. By freely exploring with a material, students will discover many of its important characteristics and will gain some understanding of where it might make sense to use it. Although some free exploration should be done during regular math time, many teachers make materials available to students during free time or before or after school.

Establishing Routines for Using Materials Establish clear expectations about how materials will be used and cared for. Consider having students suggest rules for how materials should and should not be used. Students will often be more aware of rules and policies that they have helped create.

Initially, you may need to place buckets of materials close to students as they work. Gradually, students should be expected to make decisions about what they need and to retrieve the materials on their own.

Plan for how materials will be cleaned up at the end of each class. Most teachers find that stopping 5 minutes before the end of class gives students time to clean up materials, put their work in their folders, fill out their Weekly Log, and double-check the floor for any stray materials.

Storing Materials Store manipulatives where they are easily accessible to students. Many teachers store materials in plastic tubs or shoe boxes arranged on a bookshelf or along a windowsill. In addition to pattern blocks, Geoblocks, and interlocking cubes, items such as calculators, coins, 100 charts, and paper (blank and grid) are important mathematical tools that should be available to students.

Exploring Cubes, Pattern Blocks, and Geoblocks

Materials

- Interlocking cubes (500 for 10 students)
- Pattern blocks (1 bucket per 6–8 students)
- Geoblocks (1 or 2 sets, each divided into 2–3 subsets)
- Student Sheet 3 (1 per student, homework)

What Happens

Students are introduced to pattern blocks and Geoblocks. These, in addition to the interlocking cubes, are used for free exploration. Students describe the characteristics of the three materials, noting similarities and differences. Their work focuses on:

- exploring pattern blocks
- exploring Geoblocks
- discussing attributes of interlocking cubes, pattern blocks, and Geoblocks

Activity

Exploring Pattern Blocks and Geoblocks

Introduce pattern blocks and Geoblocks as two more materials that students will be using during math class this year. As you did with the interlocking cubes, invite students to share experiences they have had with these materials.

Review ground rules for using materials that were established in Session 1 for the interlocking cubes.

For most of today and tomorrow you will be using pattern blocks, Geoblocks, and interlocking cubes. Each of these materials will be in a different part of the classroom. During the next two days everyone will have a chance to use each of the materials. You'll need to think about how to plan your time so that you have a chance to do each activity.

If there is not enough of any one material for all students to use it at the same time, you may want to set up the three materials in three different locations in the classroom. You could use tables, clusters of desks, or rug space as places for students to work. Explain to students that each "center" can accommodate a specific number of students and that sometime during the next two sessions, you would like them to be sure and spend time working with all three materials. Depending on how you've organized your classroom, this could be indicated by the number of chairs at a certain table or by posting the information on the board.

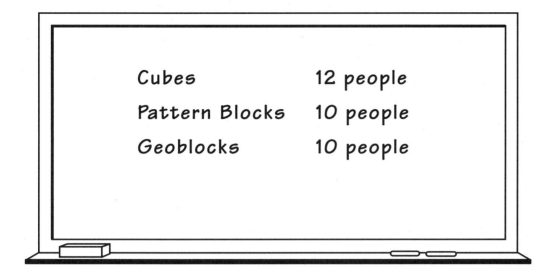

Cubes   12 people

Pattern Blocks   10 people

Geoblocks   10 people

Allow most of the class period for students to explore these materials. At the end of each session, gather students together for a short discussion about these materials.

Observing the Students Use this time as an opportunity to gather information about how students are thinking about and interacting with the materials. Do not be too concerned about their lack of knowledge or experience at this point. This session is just an introduction; there will be more directed explorations in later sessions. See About the Assessment in This Unit (p. I-20) for suggestions on assessing students and for questions you can ask yourself about students' understanding during each investigation.

Observe students as they work.

■ Do they tend to stick with the same activity for a period of time, or do they move from place to place?

■ Do they work alone or in pairs? Do they talk to others about what they are doing?

■ How do they describe the blocks? In the case of the pattern blocks, do they refer to them by shape or by color?

■ With the pattern blocks and interlocking cubes, do they build up or are their designs flat?

■ Are their constructions at all symmetrical?

■ With both the Geoblocks and pattern blocks, is there any sense that pairs or combinations of blocks can be substituted for other blocks (for example, two trapezoids will make one hexagon)?

About 20 minutes from the end of each session, ask students to clean up, and remind them where materials should be stored. A "5 minutes until cleanup" warning prepares students for the transition and helps them plan how to finish what they are involved in. Remind students to check the floor for stray materials, and ask them to help return materials to their proper storage places.

Activity

Class Discussion: What Did You Discover?

At the end of Session 2, discuss with students what they did with the cubes, pattern blocks, and Geoblocks. Some ways to approach the discussion are:

- **What material did you use and what did you do with it?**
- **Did you work alone or with a partner?**
- **Tell us about some of the blocks you used. What did you notice about them?**
- **Did you build something that went up, or did it lie flat?**

At the end of Session 3, discuss with students what they noticed about the three materials. Remind them of some of their observations about the interlocking cubes from Session 1. The following questions can begin or extend the discussion.

- **What did you notice about the pattern blocks? about the Geoblocks?**
- **Is there anything that is the same about the cubes, pattern blocks, and Geoblocks? Is there anything different?**

Classroom discussions where every student shares what he or she did can become long and difficult for many students to attend to. One way to vary discussions is by asking a few students to share what they did with a material (or how they solved a problem) and then ask the others to think about how what they did was similar to that which was just shared.

Tim just told us that he found many different ways to build the long, rectangular, solid Geoblock. Did anyone else discover that? Who discovered something different?

Trini used the pattern blocks to build walls and towers. Who else built up with the pattern blocks? Did any one just use the blocks flat on the table? Tell us about that.

As you observe students while they are working, identify two or three students who are using the materials in an interesting way. You might begin your discussion with these students.

Weekly Logs

At the end of each session, give students a few minutes to record the day's activity in their Weekly Logs. Write Exploring Cubes, Pattern Blocks, and Geoblocks on the board. Remind them to include only the materials that they have actually spent time exploring that day.

Sessions 2 and 3 Follow-Up

 **Homework**

What Is Mathematics? Students write or draw their response to the question "What is mathematics?" on Student Sheet 3.

D I A L O G U E B O X

Exploring Materials

Students need many opportunities throughout the year to freely explore materials. The teacher plays a critical role in this process. You can learn much about students by observing them as they use materials.

Students will vary in the amount of structure and direction they need as they explore. Guiding students' exploration by asking questions can be an effective way of structuring a free exploration experience for some students. This can extend students' thinking about a particular material and often lead them into new ways of using a material. At the same time, you can encourage students to make choices and decisions about materials. Encourage them to work with partners or small groups, since students benefit from observing how others use materials. Inviting them to share their constructions and designs is a natural way for them to exchange ideas.

This discussion occurred during the free exploration activities (p. 10). The teacher joins a small group of students working with pattern blocks.

Lionel: Mine is a sailboat, Here's the boat part, and then I made the mast with the skinny diamonds, and the sail is made with green triangles.

Carla: Mine is just a design. I started with this hexagon in the middle, and then I built out and around. And now it looks like a pinwheel.

Your design is similar to Phoebe's design, but she started with two red trapezoids in the center.

Carla: It's the same thing, because we just used two of these [*indicating trapezoids*] instead of this [*pointing to the hexagon*].

Graham: Stop shaking the table! I don't want my wall to fall down. It's very fragile and shaky!

I can see that some of you have decided to use the pattern blocks flat on the table and some of you have used them to build up—sort of like blocks.

The conversation is interrupted by some commotion at a table of students using interlocking cubes. Three students are building elaborate constructions and two are being silly, sliding blocks back and forth across the table.

Paul and Angel, have you figured out how to snap these cubes together so that they make a flat square? I noticed that yesterday, when you were working with the Geoblocks, you were trying to build a very tall skyscraper. Do you suppose there's a way to use these cubes to build a tall, skinny building?

Paul: Well, you could put them together in a long line like this. [*He snaps together a row of seven cubes.*]

Angel: You could make it fatter by adding more cubes on the bottom. [*She builds a two-by-two square and then begins to attach more cubes on top of her base.*]

I wonder how many floors your building could have. I live in an apartment building that has six floors.

Paul: My building has 11 floors. I'm going to make a building with 11 floors.

The teacher remains with the two students for a few more minutes, then turns her attention to the other three students in the group as Paul and Angel begin to build their buildings.

Building and Sorting Cube Things

What Happens

Students count out 30 cubes and use them to build a Cube Thing. They share their Cube Things and sort them in several ways. Their work focuses on:

■ counting a set of objects
■ sorting by similar attributes

Materials

■ Interlocking cubes (at least 30 per student)
■ Index cards or paper (1 per student)

Activity

Distribute boxes/bins of interlocking cubes to each group of students. Each student counts out 30 cubes, putting any extras back in the box. As students are counting out their 30 cubes, observe their methods of counting and checking their count.

■ Are they counting by 1's or 2's?
■ Do they count out groups of 5 or 10 cubes?
■ Do they check their count?

Without attaching your 30 cubes, organize them in some way so that it is easy to count them and see that there are exactly 30 cubes. When you have finished, share your arrangement with partners. You and your partner should check each other's count.

Circulate around the classroom and observe students' methods for organizing and arranging their cubes. Students share their arrangements with their partners, each one checking the other's count.

Discuss how students arranged their cubes. Some may have grouped their cubes into piles of 5 or 10. Others may have made a long line of 30 cubes. You may want to record their strategies on the board.

Think of something you want to build with your 30 cubes. It might be an animal, a toy, or something else. You may need a few more cubes or a few less to build your "Cube Thing." It's okay to use a few more or a few less than 30. However, when you are finished building, you should know exactly how many cubes you used. Make sure that you build it so it is sturdy—it should stay together when it is picked up or moved.

Building Cube Things

Note: You may wish to set guidelines ahead of time about the types of objects students can build; for example, no weapons.

Walk around and observe students while they work. You may need to help some students who are having difficulty attaching the cubes to one another. Remind students that they are to use about 30 cubes and they need to know exactly the number they used.

After about 15 minutes, distribute an index card to each student. Ask them to write their name, what they built, and the number of cubes they used to build it on the card, then stick the card in their Cube Thing.

❖ **Tip for the Linguistically Diverse Classroom** Students who are not writing comfortably in English might draw a picture of the object they built on the card. Students might add words to their drawings by getting help from partners who are more proficient in English.

Sorting Cube Things

Ask students to bring their Cube Things and cards to their desks or to the meeting place. Quickly go around the room and have students show and tell the class what they made. In this activity, categories will be based on how each student identifies his or her Cube Thing, such as "a car," rather than on numerical arrangements or color combinations of the cubes. See the **Dialogue Box**, Sorting Cube Things (p. 18), for an illustration of how one teacher worked with her class.

Select about three of the things that could belong to the same group, and place them on a table or in the center of the rug. Ask students how they are alike.

We're going to identify categories, or names, that describe some of the Cube Things. I'm going to pick some of your Cube Things that I think go together and put them on the table. Tory, bring your racing car to the table. Simon, bring up your wagon, and Rosie, bring up your tricycle. How are these things alike? What is a category or name that could describe the Cube Things in this group?

List different responses on the board. Some students may say they all move, others that they are all kinds of transportation. Choose one category from the list. Ask if any other students have made a Cube Thing that belongs in the same group and to tell why it fits in.

Let's look around the room and see if anyone else's Cube Thing belongs to the group HAS WHEELS. Who has a thing that could go on the table with these three?

Add other students' things if the class agrees that they go with the group on the table. As each new thing is added, students can check whether it fits.

Repeat the activity a few more times using different categories. You may want to vary the activity by having students identify a category before any things are selected.

After doing the activity several times, discuss how different things belonged to several groups. For example, a bicycle could belong to the group of THINGS WITH WHEELS and also to the group of THINGS YOU SIT ON. At this point, focus on categorizing by single attributes rather than overlapping groups.

When you have completed the activity, you may want to look at the number of cubes in the Cube Things by having students group together all things built from the same number of cubes, or by placing the Cube Things in order from fewest to most cubes.

At the end of the session, students take apart their Cube Things and return the cubes to the storage bins. Review how students are to clean up and where materials should be stored. Some students may be reluctant to disassemble their things. Suggest that they draw a picture of their Cube Thing on the back of the card they used to label it. This can be kept in their math folder for future reference. During the next few days, students can build more Cube Things as one of their choices.

Remind students to fill in their Weekly Logs.

Sorting Cube Things

The sorting process involves looking at objects and identifying ways that they are similar or not similar. To sort objects into categories, you often focus on certain characteristics and ignore others. For a category to be meaningful, it must include some things and exclude others.

Throughout the grade 2 *Investigations* curriculum, students will be sorting and classifying. In this first experience, focus on identifying and describing one category at a time. Students should think about possible categories for their Cube Things, then decide which category their Cube Thing belongs in.

In this discussion, the class is sorting their Cube Things (p. 16). The teacher acknowledges student comments that do not extend the discussion and refocuses the class on the task of naming a category that describes the group. Students describe what they made:

robot	skyscraper	table
dog	magic carpet	house
staircase	hallway	jet
rainbow	camera	bridge
person	sled	bed
helicopter	car	telescope
building	bird	train
turtle	dragon	castle

[The teacher asks that the house, skyscraper, and building be brought up to the front of the room.]

What's the same about a house, a skyscraper, and a building? How are they alike?

Ayaz: You build them.

Helena: People live in them.

[The teacher records these ideas on the board.]

SkySkraper brige bulding House

Continued on next page

Linda: They all have yellow in them.

Yes, they all have yellow cubes in them, but now we're trying to find a category that describes what these objects are rather than how they are made.

Ping: They're all buildings.

Simon called his Cube Thing a building. Could the other two shapes also be called buildings?

We have three categories on the board that describe all three Cube Things. Let's think a little more about what Ping just said. [*She circles "building" on the board.*] **Has anyone else made a Cube Thing that belongs to the group buildings?**

Harris: My staircase goes in a building.

Yes, many buildings have stairs, but is a staircase a building?

Harris: No. Can we change the category to THINGS IN A BUILDING?

We could, but we want to think first about the category we just identified. Is anyone else's Cube Thing a building?

Laura: Mine is. It's a castle.

[The castle is placed with the other three Cube Things. Students decide that no one else has a Cube Thing that fits the category BUILDINGS. Students who made these remove them from the front.]

Let's try another group. This time I'll name the category first. Then we'll see which Cube Things belong in it.

[The teacher looks around the room.] **I see that some of the things you made have eyes. Which Cube Things belong in this group?**

Students suggest bird, turtle, person, and robot.

Karina: Maybe Olga should put her telescope in that group. You look through it with your eye.

Olga: Well, you use your eyes for a telescope but the telescope doesn't *have* eyes like all these things.

I see two more Cube Things that I think have eyes. Can anyone find them?

[Students add the dog and the dragon.]

Now let's look at the Cube Things in this group one by one and see if they all belong together.

INVESTIGATION 2

Looking at Numbers

What Happens

Session 1: How Many Days Have We Been in School? Students are introduced to the routine, Today's Number, which will be incorporated into their school day throughout the year. They begin a class counting strip that represents the number of days they have been in school. They also record these data on a 200 chart. Students find various ways to express Today's Number using arithmetic operations.

Sessions 2 and 3: Card Games Students play two card games, Tens Go Fish and Turn Over 10. They are introduced to Choice Time activities, which they participate in for the rest of the sessions.

Sessions 4 and 5: Mystery Photos Students are introduced to two new activities, Mystery Photos and Building Cube Things. They work on these activities during Choice Time.

Session 6: Today's Number and Counting Pockets In the first half of this session, students brainstorm ways to express the number of days they have been in school. During the last half of the session, students are introduced to How Many Pockets?, the second of three ongoing classroom routines. They collect data about the number of pockets the class is wearing.

Session 7: Revealing Mystery Photos Students continue the Choice Time activities they worked on in Sessions 2–5. At the end of the session, they reveal the Mystery Photo locations and have a brief discussion about Choice Time.

Session 8: Ways to Get to 12 The book *12 Ways to Get to 11* is read to the class. Students write number sentences and identify categories for some of the situations in the book. As a class, they write and illustrate a book based on the literature,

which expresses Today's Number in a variety of ways. For homework, they choose a different number and make their own "miniversion" of a book.

Mathematical Emphasis

- Keeping track of the number of school days
- Writing equations that equal the number of days in school
- Making combinations of 10
- Identifying uses of numbers in the world

What to Plan Ahead of Time

Materials

- Index cards and adding-machine tape (Session 1)
- Interlocking cubes: at least 30 per student (Sessions 2–6)
- Resealable plastic bags or envelopes to store Mystery Photo Cards and class sets of number cards: 2 per student (Sessions 2–5)
- Chart paper or newsprint (Sessions 1, 6, 8)
- Overhead projector (Sessions 4–5)
- Large jar (Session 6)
- Masking or colored tape, or a rubber band that fits the jar (Session 6)
- *12 Ways to Get to 11* by Eve Merriam (Session 8, optional)
- Plain paper: 2 sheets per student (Sessions 2–3, 6, 8)

Other Preparation

- Duplicate the following student sheets and teaching resources (located at the end of this unit) in the following quantities. If you have Student Activity Booklets, copy only the items marked with an asterisk.

  For Session 1
  Student Sheet 4, How Do You Use Numbers? (p. 178): 1 per student (homework)

  For Sessions 2–3
  Student Sheet 5, Tens Go Fish (p. 179) and Student Sheet 6, Turn Over 10 (p. 180): 1 per student (homework), plus 6–7 for the classroom.*

  For Sessions 4–5
  Student Sheet 7, Mystery Photo Recording Sheet (p. 181): 1 per student

  Student Sheet 8, Cube Things (p. 182): 1 per pair. Cut each sheet in half.

  Mystery Photo Cards* (p. 190): 6 sets, plus overhead transparencies of three or four. Cut apart the sets and store each set in an envelope or resealable plastic bag.

  For Session 6
  Student Sheet 9, Pockets at Home (p. 183): 1 per student (homework)

  For Session 8
  Student Sheet 10, Ways to Get to _____ (p. 184): 1 per student (homework)

- Prepare a blank 200 chart by taping together two copies of the 100 chart, one above the other to form a 10-by-20 grid. Post it in a permanent place on a bulletin board or mount it on a piece of cardboard. The chart will be used throughout the year to count the number of days in school. (Session 1)

- Prepare Number of the Day cards using index cards that have been cut in half. Cut a paper strip from adding-machine tape, long enough to hold 180 number cards. Plan enough space to display the strip. (Session 1)

- If you do not have manufactured number cards from the grade 2 *Investigations* materials kit, use Number Cards (p. 186) to make one deck of number cards per pair of students for classwork. The classroom decks will last longer if duplicated on oaktag. These sets can be cut apart and stored in envelopes or plastic bags. Also duplicate enough to provide one deck per student for homework. Each deck should contain four of each number 0–10 and four wild cards. See the Materials lists with specific activities to determine whether wild cards should be included with decks each time. (Sessions 2–3)

How Many Days Have We Been in School?

Materials

- Chart paper or newsprint
- Adding-machine tape for counting strip
- Prepared Number of the Day cards
- Prepared 200 chart
- Student Sheet 4 (1 per student, homework)

What Happens

Students are introduced to the routine, Today's Number, which will be incorporated into their school day throughout the year. They begin a class counting strip that represents the number of days they have been in school. They also record these data on a 200 chart. Students find various ways to express Today's Number using arithmetic operations. Their work focuses on:

- expressing number in more than one way
- identifying where numbers are found and how they are used

Activity

Today's Number: Ways to Make 5

Today's Number is one of the routines that are built into the grade 2 *Investigations* curriculum. Routines provide students with regular practice in important mathematical ideas such as number combinations, counting and estimating data, and concepts of time. For Today's Number, which is done daily (or most days), students write equations that equal the number of days they have been in school. The complete description of Today's Number (p. 124) offers suggestions for establishing this routine and some variations.

Introduce this activity by having students look over their Weekly Log and review the activities they have worked on during math time. This can be done as a whole group or students can share with partners. Call their attention to the small box where they have been recording the number of school days.

Post a piece of chart paper on the board.

Today we have been in school for 5 days. I can show five by using a number or using a word. (Record these ways on the chart paper.)

Note: You may need to adjust the number to correspond with the number of days the students have been in school. If you do not want to use the days in school for this activity, you can use the calendar date.

Ask students to think about other ways to make five, such as number sentences. List their ideas on the chart paper. Occasionally, as students offer suggestions, ask the group if they agree with the statements. In this way, students have the opportunity to confirm an idea that they might have had or to respond to an incorrect suggestion.

❖ **Tip for the Linguistically Diverse Classroom**   For students with limited English proficiency, add pictures above the written examples on the list to show how the numbers are used. Encourage these students to use pictures to record their thoughts on the list. After a student has drawn his or her ideas, add the corresponding numbers below it.

It's important to regularly ask students to explain their thinking behind an answer, whether it is correct or incorrect—for example, How were you thinking about that problem? You might also want to have cubes available for students to check number sentences.

Students may suggest a wide range of number sentences. One of the benefits of this activity is that all students can do it at levels that are appropriate and challenging for them. It is not necessary that every student contribute a number sentence. The number sentences that students share daily will provide ideas that others will use the next day. As students grow more accustomed to this routine, they will begin to see patterns in the combinations, have favorite kinds of number sentences, or use more complicated types of expressions.

$$5$$
$$\text{five}$$
$$3 + 2$$
$$1 + 1 + 1 + 2$$
$$4 + 1$$
$$6 - 1$$
$$10 - 5$$
$$100 - 95$$
$$68 - 63$$

200 Chart and Counting Strip   Explain to students that each day they will be keeping track of the number of days in three ways: writing the number on their Weekly Log, adding the number to a class chart, and making a class counting strip (using Number of the Day cards and adding-machine tape). Also, they will list different ways to write the number, just as they did for Today's Number, 5.

Display the strip of paper you will use for the counting strip. Show the number cards you have made and post the numbers 1 through 5 in order to begin the strip. (Adjust to correspond to today's number.)

Show students the blank 200 chart and explain that another way of keeping track of the number of days in school will be by filling in this chart. Write the first five numbers on the chart. This chart can be used periodically to ask students question such as:

■ How many more days until the tenth (twentieth) day of school?
■ In 10 more days, how many days will we have been in school?
■ How many more days until the hundredth day of school?

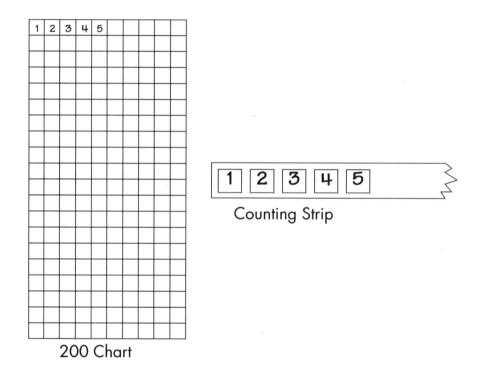

200 Chart

Counting Strip

Ways to Make 4 On a new piece of chart paper, write the number 4 (four). Distribute a sheet of blank paper to each student and have them make their own "4 chart" for yesterday's number. Working with partners, students think of all the ways they can to make 4. Each student records on his or her own 4 chart. After about 5 minutes, ask students to suggest number sentences. Record their ideas on the class chart. Post this chart next to the 5 chart. (Adjust the number so it corresponds to yesterday's number.)

Students should keep their "4 chart" in their math folder.

Uses of Numbers

Think about where you see numbers and use numbers. What are numbers for? Where do you see them?

Have the students briefly share their ideas. Ask students to complete the following sentence and record their responses on a piece of chart paper: "Numbers are used to…" or "People use numbers to…."

Students think of different uses of numbers and give examples. If students respond with a general location, such as "on a clock" or "in the store," ask them to tell what the numbers are used for, such as "to tell the time" or "to show how much something costs." If students respond only with an example of a number, such as "I am 7 years old," say, "Yes, you can use numbers to tell someone's age."

Record examples, and suggest that students continue to add to the chart as they think of other ways numbers are used.

People use numbers to:
- count
- measure
- do math
- take your temperature
- tell time

Session 1 Follow-Up

How Do You Use Numbers? Students find five ways numbers are used in their home. They also interview someone at home and ask that person to give three ways he or she uses numbers. They record the information on Student Sheet 4, How Do You Use Numbers? and bring the list to school. Tomorrow they will add any new uses of numbers they have found to the class list.

 **Homework**

❖ **Tip for the Linguistically Diverse Classroom** Students can make a pictorial list to record ways numbers are used in their homes. As they interview family members, students can draw a star next to any examples that family members suggest.

Card Games

Materials

- Number Cards, see specific activities as to whether to include wild cards (1 deck per pair; 1 deck per student, homework)
- Envelopes or resealable plastic bags (1 per student)
- Student Sheet 5 (1 per student, homework, plus 6–7 for the classroom)
- Student Sheet 6 (1 per student, homework, plus 6–7 for the classroom)
- Plain paper (2 sheets per student)
- Interlocking cubes

What Happens

Students play two card games, Tens Go Fish and Turn Over 10. They are introduced to Choice Time activities, which they participate in for the rest of the sessions. Their work focuses on:

- making 10 with two or more addends
- comparing two quantities and finding the difference
- counting a set of objects
- counting two sets of objects

Start-Up

Uses of Numbers   Students share the uses of numbers they discussed with their families for homework. Add the new uses to the list started yesterday.

Today's Number   Sometime during the school day, students brainstorm ways to express the number of days they have been in school. They add a card to the class counting strip and fill in another number on the blank 200 chart. For full directions on this routine, see p. 124.

Activity

Tens Go Fish

Tens Go Fish and Turn Over 10 are two card games that reinforce combinations of 10 with two or more addends. These can be taught to the whole class, or you might want to teach a small group of students and then have them teach other students. Try to teach both of these games during the first half of Session 2. These are two choice activities for students to work on during the remainder of Session 2 and all of Session 3.

Note: If you have duplicated the Number Cards on paper instead of card stock, have students make a "card holder" so they won't be able to see through the cards. Fold one long edge of a sheet of 8½"-by-11" paper up approximately 1 inch from the bottom to form a "pocket." Then fold the paper in half the long way, matching the bottom of the pocket with the other long edge. The paper can stand, forming a tent. Staple each side of the pocket. Slide cards into the pocket.

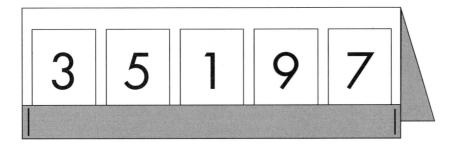

Finished size ≈ 3" by 11"

If students are familiar with the basic card game, Go Fish, they will probably need just a brief introduction to this game. If this is a new game for students, you might want to have a small group play a demonstration game in front of the class. For Tens Go Fish, remove the wild cards from the deck.

Today we will learn another way to play Go Fish. This game is called Tens Go Fish. The object of this game is to find pairs of cards that add to 10. For example, which card would you pair with the 7 card to make 10?

Each player is dealt five cards. You might be dealt two cards that equal 10, but most of the time you will have to ask someone else if he or she has a certain card. If I were holding these cards: 0, 2, 4, 5, and 7 [*write these numbers on the board*], would I have a pair that totals 10?

At my turn, I can ask another player for a card. For example, I would like to use my 2 card to make a 10. What card should I ask the other player for? So, if I were playing with Trini, I might ask, "Trini, do you have an 8?" If Trini has an 8, she gives it to me. I put the 8 and the 2 down as a pair, take a card from the deck, and my turn is over. If Trini does not have an 8, she says "Go Fish." I take a card from the deck and my turn is over, even if I pick the card I asked for.

Explain that the game continues with each player trying to make combinations of 10. If at any time, a player is holding two cards that total 10, he or she can put them down, without drawing another card. The game is over when there are no more cards to draw. At the end of the game, each player makes a list on a sheet of paper of the pairs of cards he or she has. Players label this list Tens Go Fish, write the date on the top, and put it in their math folder. Model this procedure for students.

This is another way that you and the students can keep track of their activity during Choice Time.

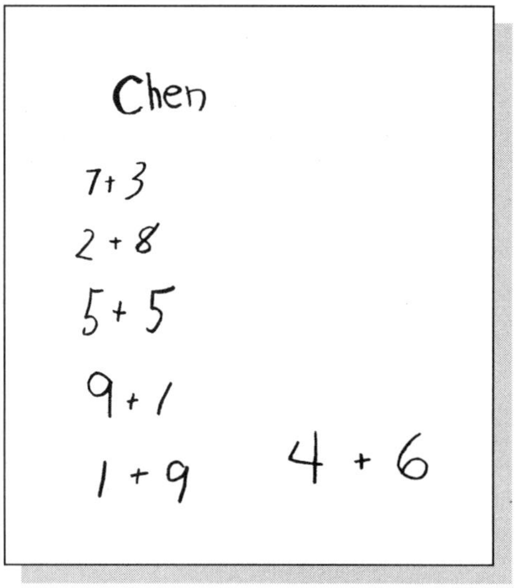

Chen

7 + 3
2 + 8
5 + 5
9 + 1
1 + 9   4 + 6

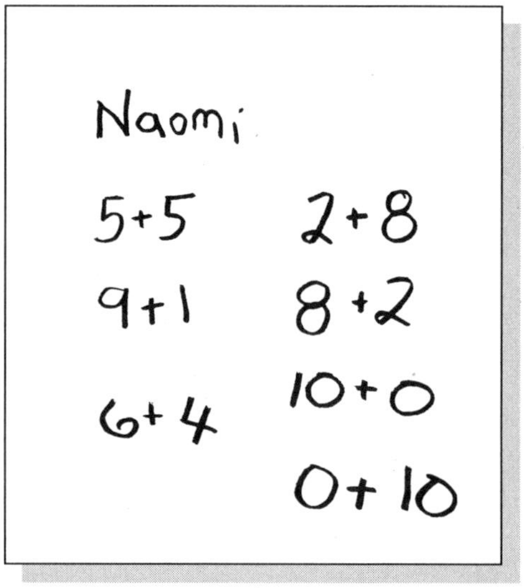

Naomi

5 + 5   2 + 8
9 + 1   8 + 2
6 + 4   10 + 0
          0 + 10

Depending on how much time is left in this session, you may want to have everyone in your class play a game of Tens Go Fish and introduce Turn Over 10 in the next session.

Note: You may want to suggest that students use 10 cubes to help them find combinations of 10.

Turn Over 10

This is another card game that involves making combinations of 10. While Tens Go Fish uses combinations of two addends, in Turn Over 10 students make combinations of 10 using two or *more* addends. Players also use the wild cards in Turn Over 10.

The easiest way to introduce this game is by assembling students in a circle on the floor and playing a demonstration game in the middle of the circle.

This game is called Turn Over 10. You will be using all of the cards in the deck, including the wild cards. A wild card is a special card because whoever turns it over can decide how much it is worth, depending on what is needed. To begin this game, arrange the cards face down in four rows with five cards in each row.

Arrange the cards. Pause and ask students to figure out how many cards there are. Notice how students figure out the total number of cards. Do they count each card by 1's? Do they count by 5's? Do they add 2 rows of 5 and then add 10 plus 10? Ask a few students to share their strategies.

Explain to students that the object of this game is to turn over cards that total 10. Ask one student to play with you and demonstrate a few rounds in front of the class.

Turn over two cards. As you play, involve students in your turn.

I turned over a 3 and a 4. What card could I turn over next to make exactly 10? What cards could I turn over and make less than 10? If I turn over a wild card what number should I make it into?

If a player gets a total of 10, he or she takes the cards, then replaces them with cards from the deck. The player gets another turn.

Demonstrate how cards from the deck are used to replace the cards that are taken when a total of 10 is made. You probably will not need to complete an entire demonstration game. Make sure, however, that students understand that the game is over when no more combinations of 10 can be made. At the end of the game, each player should record his or her combinations in a way similar to Tens Go Fish. Students can write the name of the game, the date, and the combinations of cards they made.

Introducing Choice Time

Explain to students that in math class they often will be working on Choice Time activities. This means they will have to choose which of several different activities they will work on.

Choice Time is a format that recurs throughout the *Investigations* curriculum. See the **Teacher Note**, About Choice Time (p. 32), for information about how to set up Choice Time activities, including how students use their Weekly Log to keep track of their work.

Tell students that during each day of Choice Time activities, they choose one or two of the activities they want to participate in. They can select the same activity more than once but should not go to the same activity each day. Decide if you want students to try every activity or just some of them.

List these choices on the chalkboard. You may want to have a few extra copies of the game directions (Student Sheets 5 and 6) available for students to refer to as they play.

> 1. Tens Go Fish
>
> 2. Turn Over 10

Choice 1: Tens Go Fish

Materials: Deck of Number Cards 0–10 (no wild cards) for each group of 2–3 players

Each player is dealt five cards. Players take turns asking each other for cards that, when combined with a card in their hand, will total 10. If a player makes a combination of 10, those cards are placed on the table, a new card is drawn from the deck, and the player's turn is over. If a player cannot make a combination of 10, a card is drawn from the deck. If the player draws the card he or she requested, the player can put down the matching pair, then the turn is over. The game is over when there are no cards left in the deck. At the end of the game each player makes a list of the combinations of 10 that he or she collected.

Choice 2: Turn Over 10

Materials: Deck of Number Cards 0 to 10 including four wild cards for each group of 2–3 players

Arrange the cards face down in four rows of five. The remaining cards are placed face down in a pile. Players take turns trying to turn over cards that total 10. If the total is more than 10, the turn is over and the cards are turned face down again. If the total is exactly 10, players take the cards and replace the missing cards with cards from the deck, then take another turn. The game is over when no more 10's can be made. At the end of the game each player records the combinations of 10 he or she found during the game.

Observing the Students

During this first Choice Time, observe for the following:

Do students try each choice, or do they stay with a familiar one? If, after a short time with one activity, students say they're done, ask them to tell you about what they have done and encourage them to investigate further. Do students work alone or with partners? Do they share what they have done with others and observe what others are doing? Do they talk to themselves or others about what they are doing?

Below are some specific suggestions of what you might observe as students play the two card games. These two activities, in addition to Building Cube Things, which is introduced in the next session, focus on combinations of numbers and on counting.

Tens Go Fish

- Do students easily identify pairs of 10? How do they decide which card to ask for?

- To find a sum of 10, do students use cubes? Do they count on from the number they have? Do they just "know" the pairs of numbers that make 10?

- Are students able to keep track of the cards other players have asked for?

Turn Over 10

- How do students keep track of the total they have turned over?

- Are students able to predict which card they need to make a total of 10?

- Are students able to keep track of the position of numbers, or do they randomly turn over cards?

- How do students use wild cards to complete their 10 or to extend their turn?

Near the End of the Session   Five or ten minutes before the end of each Choice Time, have students stop working, put away the materials they have been working with, and clean up their work area.

When cleanup is complete, students should record what they worked on during Choice Time on their Weekly Logs (Student Sheet 1). Suggest that they use the list of Choice Time activities that you posted as a reference.

Whenever possible, either at the beginning or end of Choice Time, have students share the work they have been doing. This often sparks interest in an activity. Some days you might ask two or three students to share with the class the work they have been doing. On other days you might ask a question that came up during Choice Time so that others might respond to it. Sometimes you might want students to explain how they thought about or solved a particular problem.

Sessions 2 and 3 Follow-Up

Playing Card Games at Home   After Session 3, students play one of the card games with someone at home. Each student will need a set of Number Cards, which they can cut up at home, and directions for the game they have chosen to teach their family (Student Sheet 5, Tens Go Fish, or Student Sheet 6, Turn Over 10). Students will be playing the other game after Sessions 4 and 5, so you may want to send directions for both games home tonight. You also may want to provide an envelope for them to keep their set of Number Cards in. Suggest that students keep these cards in a special place because they will be playing these games and other card games for homework throughout the unit.

 **Homework**

Choice Time is an opportunity for students to work on a variety of activities that focus on similar mathematical content. Choice Time activities are found in most units of the grade 2 *Investigations* curriculum. These generally alternate with whole-class activities in which students work individually or in pairs on one or two problems. Each format offers different classroom experiences. Both are important for students to be engaged in.

In Choice Time the activities are not sequential; as students move among them, they continually revisit some of the important concepts and ideas they are learning. Many Choice Time activities are designed with the intent that students will work on them more than once. By playing a game a second or third time or solving similar problems, students are able to refine strategies, see a variety of approaches, and bring new knowledge to familiar experiences.

You may want to limit the number of students who work on a Choice Time activity at one time. Often when a new choice is introduced, many students want to do it first. Assure them that they will be able to try each choice. In many cases, the quantity of materials available limits the number of students who can do an activity at any one time. Even if this is not the case, set guidelines about the number of students who work on each choice. This gives students the opportunity to work in smaller groups and to make decisions about what they want and need to do. It also provides a chance to do some choices more than once.

Initially you may need to help students plan what they do. Rather than organizing them into groups and circulating the groups every 15 minutes, support students in making decisions about the choices they do. Making choices, planning their time, and taking responsibility for their own learning are important aspects of a student's school experience. If some students return to the same activity over and over again without trying other choices, suggest that they make a different first choice and then choose the favorite activity as a second choice.

How to Set Up Choices

Some teachers prefer to have choices set up at centers or stations around the room. At each center, students will find the materials needed to complete the activity. Other teachers prefer to have materials stored in a central location and have students bring materials to their desks or tables. In either case, materials should be readily accessible to students, and students should be expected to take responsibility for cleaning up and returning materials to their appropriate storage locations. Giving students a "5 minutes until cleanup" warning before the end of an activity session allows them to finish what they are working on and prepare for the upcoming transition.

You may also find that you need to experiment with a few different structures before finding a setup that works best for you and your students.

The Role of the Student

Establish clear guidelines when you introduce Choice Time activities. Discuss students' respon-sibilities:

■ Try every choice at least once.

■ Work with partners or alone. (Some activities require that students work in pairs, while others can be done either alone or with partners.)

■ Keep track, on paper, of the choices you have worked on.

■ Keep all your work in your math folder.

■ Ask questions of other students when you don't understand or feel stuck. (Some teachers establish the rule, "Ask two other students before me," requiring students to check with two peers before coming to the teacher for help.)

Students can use their Weekly Logs to keep track of their work. As students finish a choice, they

Continued on next page

write it on their log and place any work they have done in their folder. Some teachers list the choices for sessions on a chart, the board, or the overhead projector to help students keep track of what they need to do.

In any classroom there will be a range of how much work students complete. Some choices include extensions and additional problems for students to do when they have completed their required work. Encourage students to return to choices they have done before, do another problem or two from the choice, or play a game again.

At the end of a Choice Time session, spend a few minutes discussing with students what went smoothly, what sorts of issues arose and how they were resolved, and what students enjoyed or found difficult. Encourage students to be involved in the process of finding solutions to problems that come up in the classroom. In doing so, they take some responsibility for their own behavior and become involved with establishing classroom policies. You may also want to make the choices available at other times during the day.

The Role of the Teacher

Choice Time provides you with the opportunity to observe and listen to students while they work. At times, you may want to meet with individual students, pairs, or small groups who need help or whom you haven't had a chance to observe before, or to do individual assessments. Recording your observations of students will help you keep track of how they are interacting with materials and solving problems. The **Teacher Note,** Keeping Track of Students' Work (p. 34), offers some strategies for recording and using observations of students.

You will probably find that much of your time during the initial weeks of Choice Time is spent circulating around the classroom helping students get settled into activities and monitoring the overall management of the classroom. Once routines are familiar and well established, students will become more independent and responsible for their work during Choice Time. This will allow you to spend more concentrated periods of time observing the class as a whole or working with individuals and small groups.

Throughout the *Investigations* curriculum, there are numerous opportunities to observe students as they work. Teacher observations are an important part of ongoing assessment. While individual observations are snapshots of a student's experience with a single activity, when considered over time they can provide an informative and detailed picture. These observations can be useful in documenting and assessing a student's growth. They offer important sources of information when preparing for family conferences or writing student reports.

Your observations of students will vary throughout the year. At times you may be interested in particular strategies that students are developing to solve problems. You might want to observe how students are using materials to help them solve problems. Or you may be interested in noting the strategy that a student uses when playing a game during Choice Time. Class discussions also provide many opportunities to take note of student ideas and thinking.

You may want to develop some sort of system to record and keep track of your observations of students. While a few ideas and suggestions are offered here, the most important aspect of developing a system of keeping track is finding one that works for you. Too often keeping observation notes on a class of 28 students can become overwhelming and time-consuming.

A class list of names is a convenient way of jotting down observations of students. Since the space is somewhat limited, it is not possible to write lengthy notes; however, when kept over time these short observations provide important information.

Stick-on address labels can be placed on clipboards around the room. Notes can be taken on individual students and then these labels can be peeled off and put in a file that has been set up for each student.

Alternatively, you may find that jotting down brief notes at the end of each week works well for you. Some teachers find that this is a useful way of reflecting on the class as a whole, on the curriculum, and on individual students. Planning for the next weeks' activities often develops from these weekly reflections.

In addition to your own notes on students, each student will be keeping a folder of work for any given unit. This work and the daily entries on the Weekly Log are also pieces of information that can document a student's experience. Together they can help you keep track of the students in your class, assess their growth over time, and communicate this information to others. At the end of each unit there is a list of things you might choose to keep in individual student portfolios.

Mystery Photos

What Happens

Students are introduced to two new activities, Mystery Photos and Building Cube Things. They work on these activities during Choice Time. Their work focuses on:

- identifying places where numbers appear
- counting a set of objects
- combining two groups of objects
- recording a strategy for combining two numbers

Start-Up

Today's Number Sometime during the school day, students brainstorm ways to express the number of days they have been in school. Add a card to the class counting strip, and fill in another number on the blank 200 chart. For full directions on this routine, see p. 124.

Materials

- Student Sheet 7 (1 per student)
- Prepared sets of Mystery Photo Cards (6 sets)
- Transparencies of several Mystery Cards
- Student Sheet 8 (cut in half, 1 per pair)
- Interlocking cubes
- Overhead projector

Mystery Photos

Introduce the new Choice Time activity.

I'm going to show you photographs of numbers in different places. The numbers are on things you see every day. You will not see the whole thing in the photo. Look at the picture, think about where the numbers might be, and raise your hand if you think you know where they are. Since we want everyone to have a chance to think about the picture before people share their ideas, please don't say the place out loud.

Show the transparency of the clock, for example Card 10. Wait until most students have their hands raised before you begin calling on them. Let several students respond. Accept all responses, and have students discuss the reasons for their answers. See the **Teacher Note**, Encouraging Thinking and Reasoning (p. 39). In addition, ask students if they can explain what the numbers indicate (hours, size, price).

Show transparencies of one or two other cards, and have students describe where they think the numbers are.

Distribute Student Sheet 7 to each student, and show them a set of Mystery Photo Cards.

In this Choice Time activity, you and a partner will figure out where the numbers in the Mystery Photo Cards can be found. Each of the cards is numbered. When you think you have figured it out, look at the number on the card, find that number on your sheet, and write what you think.

Demonstrate how to record their guesses using one or two of the Mystery Photos that you displayed on the overhead. Students will use this sheet during Choice Time, so suggest that they put it in their math folders while you introduce the next activity.

Building Cube Things

This activity is a variation of Building Cube Things that students completed in the first investigation. In this version, they grab a handful of cubes with each hand, record how many cubes were in each handful, find the total, then build a Cube Thing with the cubes.

The activity should be set up as a center for about eight students at a time. Briefly introduce this new Choice Time activity.

Last week you made Cube Things out of 30 cubes. This new activity is very similar to that. In this activity the number of cubes you can use in your Cube Thing is how many you can grab in a handful.

You will begin by grabbing a handful of cubes with your left hand. Count the cubes and record the amount on Student Sheet 8. Then grab a handful of cubes with your right hand and count and record them. Next, you will find how many cubes there are in all.

When you have recorded the total number of cubes, build a Cube Thing.

As students work on this activity, encourage them to think about different ways of finding the total. Some students may count by 1's, 2's, or 5's. Others may have strategies about adding the two numbers. Remind them to record how they figured out the total on their student sheet.

When students have completed their Cube Thing, ask them to record what they made. If possible, arrange for a place to display their structures.

Students will be working on these choices during the next three sessions:

Choice Time

```
1. Tens Go Fish

2. Turn Over 10

3. Mystery Photos

4. Cube Things
```

When new choices are added to the list, there is often a great deal of interest in trying a new activity first. You may initially need to help students plan their Choice Time activities. Assure them that they will have an opportunity to try each choice. Support students in making these decisions and plans for themselves, rather than organizing them into groups.

You might have students check with you before moving on to a new choice or at the end of a session. That will help you monitor students' work and understanding. Also, it might help students get started on choices the following day.

For a review of the descriptions of Choice 1: Tens Go Fish and Choice 2: Turn Over 10 and suggestions about what to observe as students work, see p. 30.

Choice 3: Mystery Photos

Materials: Prepared sets of Mystery Photo Cards (6 sets), Student Sheet 7, Mystery Photo Recording Sheet (1 per student)

Students work with a partner, look at all the photographs, and discuss where they think the pictures were taken. They record their answers on the recording sheet.

Choice 4: Building Cube Things

Materials: Bins of interlocking cubes, Student Sheet 8, Cube Things (1 per student)

Students grab handfuls of cubes, record how many cubes in all on Student Sheet 8, and then build a Cube Thing with these cubes. If they wish, they record what they built and draw a picture of it. Arrange for a place where students can display their Cube Things.

Observing the Students

Observe students at work and watch for the following:

Mystery Photos

■ Are students familiar with the mystery number locations? Are students able to identify how the numbers are used in these photos?

Building Cube Things

■ How do students count the number of cubes in their handfuls? by 1's? by 2's? by other groups?

■ What strategy do they use for combining their two handfuls? Do some students count all from 1? Do they count on by 1's from one number? Do they have a strategy for adding numbers mentally?

At the end of the session, after students have cleaned up their materials, remind them to record what they have done on their Weekly Log.

Sessions 4 and 5 Follow-Up

 **Homework**

More Card Games at Home   After Session 4, students teach someone at home to play either Tens Go Fish or Turn Over 10. They will need directions (Student Sheet 5 or 6) for whichever game they have not yet played at home.

Encouraging Thinking and Reasoning

The student's role in math class is an active one. Getting correct answers is not enough; students should be encouraged to think critically about their ideas, give reasons for their answers, and communicate their ideas to others. Reflecting on one's own thinking and learning is a challenge for all learners, and even the youngest students can begin to engage in this important aspect of mathematics learning.

The teacher has an important role in extending students' ideas. By asking questions or by reflecting on what a student has said, you engage not only that student but the rest of the class in thinking about an answer or statement. For example, in the activity Mystery Photos, students guess the location of numbers in photographs. By following up a student's response with "What clue in this picture makes you think this is a clock?" the student is encouraged to clarify his or her thinking. Posing a question to the whole class such as, "Who has a different idea?" extends the discussion and encourages the sharing of other ideas.

In Enough for the Class? (Investigation 4, Session 1), students share strategies for comparing two numbers. After a strategy is shared, a question such as, "Who used a strategy similar to Olga's?" encourages students to think about how their ideas are similar or different. "What different strategies did you use?" again extends the discussion and encourages a variety of responses.

Often asking "Why do you think that?" or "How do you know?" evokes the response "I just knew it" or no response at all. Sometimes reflecting back to a student, "I noticed that you made two towers of cubes when you were solving this problem" helps focus a student on his or her own process.

Reflecting on one's own thinking and considering the ideas of others evolves over time. Although young students are often egocentric in their approach to learning, they can begin to understand that an important part of doing mathematics is being able to explain your ideas and give reasons for your answers.

Today's Number and Counting Pockets

Materials

- Interlocking cubes
- Large jar
- Masking or colored tape, or a rubber band that fits the jar
- Chart paper
- Student Sheet 9 (1 per student, homework)
- Plain paper (2 sheets per student)

What Happens

In the first half of this session, students brainstorm ways to express the number of days they have been in school. During the last half of the session, students are introduced to How Many Pockets?, the second of three ongoing classroom routines. They collect data about the numbers of pockets the class is wearing. Their work focuses on:

- expressing number in more than one way
- counting a group of objects in more than one way
- collecting data

Start-Up

Playing Card Games at Home At the beginning of class, briefly check in with students about their experiences teaching Tens Go Fish or Turn Over 10 to someone at home. Remind students that they should keep their playing cards and directions in a safe place at home because they will need them for future homework assignments.

Activity

Today's Number

For the first 15 minutes of this session, students generate number sentences or expressions that represent the number of the day.

Distribute paper to students and have them write today's date and the number of the day at the top of the page. As a class, generate three or four expressions, such as 6 + 4, for Today's Number. Record these on the board or a sheet of chart paper. Students then work with partners to record other expressions that equal the number of the day on their paper. As students are working, circulate around the class to get a sense of how students are doing with this activity.

After about 5 minutes, call the group together and record expressions on the class chart. The **Dialogue Box,** Patterns in Addition (p. 45), provides some examples of the range of responses offered in one second grade classroom. Some students may want to add new expressions to their list, based on classmates' contributions. Ask students to draw a line under the expressions they found and to record new expressions under the line. In this way, you can get a clearer sense of how individual students approached this task.

Students should save these papers in their math folders. Every so often you might choose to do Today's Number in this way. You can look at individual students' work and progress by comparing the papers over time.

How Many Pockets?

The routine How Many Pockets? gives students an opportunity to collect, represent, and interpret numerical data through an experience that is meaningful to them. As students collect data about pockets throughout the year, they create natural opportunities to compare quantities and to see that data can change over time.

How Many Pockets? is one of the classroom routines that occur regularly throughout the *Investigations* curriculum. The complete write-up of this routine, which includes several versions, can be found at the end of this unit (p. 127). If you are doing the full-year grade 2 *Investigations* curriculum, try to collect pocket data at regular intervals throughout the year. Many teachers have chosen to collect pocket data every tenth day of school. Most likely this session, which introduces the pocket activities, will not fall exactly on your tenth day of school. Adjust the sessions to fit your schedule by either doing this activity on *your* tenth day of school or by choosing some other interval of time in which to do this routine.

Introduce the pockets routine by telling students that this year they will collect data about the total number of pockets the students in the class wear to school. Explain that about every 10 days, the class will have a Pocket Day. On that day, students will figure out how many pockets the class is wearing.

How many pockets do you think all the people in our class are wearing today?

Invite students to share their estimates and the reasons for their estimates. Some students may guess, while others may take into account the class size or the day's attendance. Record their estimates on the chalkboard or on chart paper.

Tell students that you've thought of a way of counting the pockets. Show the containers of interlocking cubes. Explain that each person should count the pockets he or she is wearing and take one cube for each pocket. Enlist a few volunteers to help pass bins of cubes around the class.

Have students re-count to make sure they have the same number of cubes as pockets. If students have difficulty determining the correct number of cubes, suggest that they put one cube in each pocket, then remove and count the cubes used. Most likely there will be some students who are not wearing pockets. To keep them involved in the activity, assign those students the number zero.

Show students the large jar, and explain that as you call out numbers, students who have that many pockets should put their cubes in the jar. Doing the procedure this way, rather than passing the jar around the group offers you an opportunity to reinforce using the cubes as a one-to-one representation of pockets.

As students share how many pockets they have, record the information on the chalkboard with tally marks.

If you have zero pockets, come to the front of the room. How many students have no pockets? How many cubes will they put in the jar?

If you have 1 (2, 3, etc.) pockets, come to the front of the room. How many students have 1 pocket? Please put your cubes in the jar.

Pockets	Students
0	III
1	HHI
2	

When all cubes have been collected, hold up or pass the jar around so that everyone can see it. Point out the list of the pocket estimates. When the jar returns to you, mark how much of the jar is filled with cubes by placing a piece of tape, or by positioning a rubber band, around the jar at that point. (Save the jar, keeping the marking intact. Students can use this visual reference when they estimate on the next Pocket Day.)

How can we count the cubes to find out exactly how many pockets we are wearing today?

At this point in the year, students are comfortable counting by 1's and are likely to suggest that strategy. Tell the group that to be sure their count is accurate, they'll need to check their counting. Explain that you want them to count in a different way to check. Together, decide on at least two different ways to count the cubes, for example by 1's, by groups of 2's, 5's, or 10's. With the whole group, count the cubes in at least two ways.

When you've found the total number of pockets the class is wearing, record it on chart paper, in a way similar to the one shown here.

How many pockets are we wearing today?		
	Pockets	People
Pocket Day 1	42	22

You might also record the pocket data and the number of people present on the class number line by tacking up an index card under the number of the day.

Today was the first time that we collected information about the number of pockets worn by the people in our classroom. In 10 more school days we will do this activity again. If today is the tenth day of school, can you predict when we collect pocket data again?

You might want to direct students' attention to the 200 chart where they have been recording the number of days in school as a resource for solving this problem.

Writing About Pockets

Periodically in the grade 2 *Investigations* curriculum, students are asked to write about some aspect of their work in math class. For example, students may write about strategies they used to solve a problem, write story problems or situations, or write about a survey they conducted with their families. In this first writing experience, students write a short report describing what happened during math class.

About 10 or 15 minutes before the end of the session, distribute paper and ask students to write about Pocket Day.

On this paper write about our first Pocket Day. As you write, answer these questions: What did we want to know? What did we do? What did we find out? Remember to tell about any materials we used and how many pockets we counted altogether. You can use words, pictures, and numbers to write about the activity.

Students will vary in their ability to express their thoughts in writing. Even the students who are the most comfortable writing may not write more than two or three sentences for this first assignment. A few students may have difficulty getting anything down on paper. It may be helpful to ask probing questions, such as "What did we want to find out?" and "What happened next?" and then urge students to write their responses.

When everyone has finished, ask several students to read and share what they wrote.

❖ **Tip for the Linguistically Diverse Classroom** Students with a limited English proficiency can divide their paper into three sections. Ask students to draw a picture at the top of each section to represent the question to be answered. Then have students draw their responses to the questions. For example,

Section 1: Draw a question mark to represent *What did we want to know?*

Section 2: Draw a cube to represent *What did we do?*

Section 3: Draw a pocket to represent *What did we find out?*

Session 6 Follow-Up

 **Homework**

Pockets at Home Students share what they did during Pocket Day with their families. They count the pockets on people in their families. Suggest that students ask family members to guess the total number of pockets before the data are totaled. Students record their pocket data on Student Sheet 9, Pockets at Home.

Patterns in Addition

During the activity Today's Number (p. 40), this class focuses on the number 10. The students draw from their experiences with the games Tens Go Fish and Turn Over 10 as they find combinations for 10.

The teacher focuses the group on looking at combinations of 10 using two addends. Students are asked how they can be sure they have found all the combinations, which sets the stage for possibly discovering an important number pattern. The following number sentences are listed on chart paper:

	10	
5 + 5	10 + 0	22 − 12
30 − 20	18 − 8	9 + 1
7 + 3	1 + 9	15 − 5
10 + 10 − 10		
4 + 3 + 2 + 1		
2 + 2 + 2 + 2 + 2		

You've found different ways to make 10. Let's look at just the number sentences that add two numbers, for example 5 + 5. Do you see or know any others? [*Teacher begins to make a separate list of these combinations.*]

Ayaz: There's 10 + 0 and 9 + 1 and 7 + 3. Those are on our list already.

Laura: There's 1 + 9, too.

Rosie: Isn't that a repeat, the same as 9 + 1?

Ayaz: Well, yes and no, I think. I think you should write it next to 9 + 1.

We talked about similar combinations the other day when we were finding ways to make 8. Some students thought they were the same and others thought they were different. Ayaz, your idea of writing them next to each other is a good one. OK, are there any others?

Harris: 6 + 4 makes 10 and so does 4 + 6.

Karina: You can also add 0 + 10.

So, do you think we have found all the combinations of two numbers that make 10? How could we be sure that we have them all?

Camilla: I think I see something about the numbers. It goes down from 10 then 9 then 7 and 6.

Ebony: I think there's something missing because it's like a pattern, but you need an 8 in there between the 9 and the 7. It would be 8 + 2.

[The teacher writes 8 + 2 under 9 + 1.]

Tim: And you need 2 + 8, too, on the other side.

Camilla: Now see the pattern I meant? The numbers on one side go down and on the other side go up. See, it's like if you had some cubes [*she takes 10 cubes from the bin on her table*] and you made two groups. Like 9 over here and then 1. Then if you make a group of 8, this one is less, but this group is more because it goes from 1 to 2.

Salim: And if you put the 5 + 5 under the 6 + 4, then that's sort of where the pattern turns and goes the other way. So I think we have them all.

So some of you are seeing a pattern with these combinations of 10. How many people think that we have found them all? How many aren't sure? I'm going to leave this chart here for a couple of days, and I'd like you to keep thinking about the pattern that Camilla and Salim noticed. If you discover another combination of 10 using two numbers, let us know and we will add it to the list.

10 + 0	0 + 10
9 + 1	1 + 9
8 + 2	2 + 8
7 + 3	3 + 7
6 + 4	4 + 6
5 + 5	

Revealing Mystery Photos

Materials

All materials for this session have been gathered and prepared in previous sessions.

- Materials for Tens Go Fish
- Materials for Turn Over 10
- Materials for Cube Things
- Prepared sets of Mystery Photo Cards (6 sets)
- Student Sheet 7 (1 for each student)

What Happens

Students continue the Choice Time activities they worked on in Sessions 2–5. At the end of the session, they reveal the Mystery Photo locations and have a brief discussion about Choice Time. Their work focuses on:

- identifying places where numbers appear
- counting a set of objects
- combining two groups of objects
- recording strategies for combining two numbers

Start-Up

Pockets at Home Students share the pocket data they collected for homework. How many people did they survey at home? What was the total number of pockets they counted? Who counted the most (fewest) pockets? For full directions on this activity, see p. 127.

Today's Number Sometime during the school day, students brainstorm ways to express the number of days they have been in school. Add a card to the class counting strip and fill in another number on the blank 200 chart. For full directions on this activity, see p. 124.

Activity

Choice Time

Students work on activity choices during the first part of the session. Refer to previous Choice Time activities for materials and setup information, and suggestions on what to watch for as you observe students.

Toward the end of Choice Time, ask a few students to put all the sets of Mystery Photos in order (from 1–16) in preparation for the next activity.

1. Tens Go Fish
2. Turn Over 10
3. Mystery Photos
4. Cube Things

Revealing Mystery Photos

During the last 10 or 15 minutes of the session, gather the students together with their copies of Student Sheet 7, Mystery Photo Recording Sheet. Distribute the sets of Mystery Photos so that every four to six students share a set. Have students check to see that the photos are in numerical order.

Quickly go through the set of photos and have students share answers to these questions:

- **Where was the photo taken?**
- **What do the numbers in the photo mean?**

Compare the words students use to identify the locations of the photos. Which are different words for the same or similar locations? If students disagree about any of the photos, have them share the reasons for their answers.

If there is time at the end of the session, students discuss how they worked during Choice Time.

- **Which Choice Time activities did you enjoy? Why?**
- **How did you work with others during Choice Time?**

You may find that students will benefit by continuing to do some of the choice activities over time. See the **Teacher Note**, Collaborating with the Authors (p. 48), for more about your role in making the *Investigations* curriculum meet the needs of students.

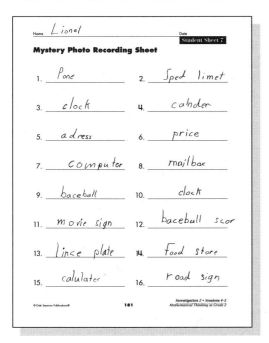

Collaborating with the Authors

Every unit in this curriculum is a guide, not a prescription or a recipe. We tested these activities in many different classrooms, representing a range of students and teachers, and we revised our ideas constantly as we learned from students and teachers alike. Each time we tried a curriculum unit in a classroom, no matter how many times it had been tried and revised before, we discovered new ideas we wanted to add and changes we wanted to make. This process could be endless, and so we had to stop and decide that the curriculum works well for a wide range of students.

We cannot anticipate the needs and strengths of your particular students this particular year. We believe that the only way for a good curriculum to be used well is for teachers to be active participants in continually modifying it. Your role is to observe and listen carefully to your students, to try to understand how they are thinking, and to make decisions, based on these observations, about what they need next. Modifications to the curriculum that you will need to consider throughout the year include the following:

- changing the numbers in a problem to make the problem more accessible or more challenging for particular students

- repeating activities with which students need more experience

- engaging students in extensions and further questions

- rearranging pairs or small groups so that students learn from a variety of their peers

Your students can help you set the right level of pace and challenge. We have found that, when given choices of activities and problems, students often do choose the right level of difficulty for themselves. You can encourage students to do this by urging them to find problems that are "not too easy, not too hard, but just right." Help students understand that doing mathematics does *not* mean knowing the answer right away. Tell students often, "A good problem for you is a problem that makes you think hard and work hard. You might have to try more than one way of doing it before you figure it out."

The *Investigations* curriculum provides more than enough material for any student. Suggestions are included for extending activities, and some curriculum units contain optional sessions (called Excursions) to provide more opportunities to explore the big mathematical ideas of that unit. Many teachers also have favorite activities that they integrate into this curriculum. We encourage you to be an active partner with us in creating the way this curriculum can work best for your students.

Ways to Get to 12

What Happens

The book *12 Ways to Get to 11* is read to the class. Students write number sentences and identify categories for some of the situations in the book. As a class, they write and illustrate a book based on the literature that expresses Today's Number in a variety of ways. For homework, they choose a different number and make their own "miniversion" of a book.

- writing equations to match situations in a book
- expressing a number using a variety of number sentences
- identifying categories for different situations

Start-Up

Today's Number Sometime during the school day, students brainstorm ways to express the number of days they have been in school. Add a card to the class counting strip and fill in another number on the blank 200 chart. See p. 124 for full directions on this routine.

Materials

- *12 Ways to Get to 11* by Eve Merriam (optional)
- Student Sheet 10 (1 per student, homework)
- Plain paper (2 sheets per student)
- Chart paper (optional)

Activity

Ways to Get to 11

12 Ways to Get to 11 illustrates different combinations of numbers that total 11. Each page focuses on a different category or group of items, for example, "At the circus, six peanut shells and five pieces of popcorn." Throughout the book combinations of 11 are given using two to four addends.

Introduce and read the book *12 Ways to Get to 11*. Each combination of 11 objects has a common theme. If you do not have the book, make up some situations and think of groups of things within that situation that you can use as examples to illustrate the idea.

I'm going to read part of the book again. On each page, we'll stop after I read it, name a category, and write a number sentence to go with the situation.

[*Read the first situation.*] **"Pick up nine pine cones from the forest floor and two acorns." What group or category can you think of that pine cones and acorns might be in?** (things in a forest, seeds from trees)

What number sentence describes this scene?

Read a few more examples. Choose some of the following to read:

- Magician's hat (4 + 5 + 1 + 1)
- Apple (6 + 1 + 1 + 3)
- Boat (2 + 2 [or 1 + 1] + 4 + 1 + 1 + 1)
- Babies (3 + 3 + 3 + 2)

After each example, students should describe the situation and the number sentence that it represents. Record both on the board.

Teacher Checkpoint

Ways to Get to 12

Teacher Checkpoints are places for you to stop and observe student work (for more information, see About Assessment, p. I-10). However, keep in mind that this entire unit is designed to help you assess students' understanding of mathematical ideas. See About the Assessment in This Unit (p. I-20) for detailed questions you can ask yourself about student understanding during each investigation.

We can make a class book similar to *12 Ways to Get to 11*. Since this is the [twelfth *or use today's number*] day of school, all the things in our situations will total [12] instead of 11. Suppose everyone in the class wrote about a different situation, what would be the name of our class book? What if everyone in the class worked with partners to write a situation, what would be the name of our book?

Brainstorm and list on the board some categories that might be settings for situations. Pick one and as a class write a story to go with it.

OK, we've chosen birthday party as a category to write about together. Who can think of a story with a total of 12 things in it for a party?

Record the class story on the board or chart paper. Then write a number sentence below it to illustrate the numbers in the story.

Distribute paper to the class. Students, individually or in pairs, choose a category and write a story using Today's Number of things in it. They label their stories with the category and write a number sentence to go with the story below it (or on the back of the paper). Each student should then illustrate his or her story.

If students finish early, they may want to write a story about the same category using different combinations of numbers and/or things.

Observe students while they work.

- How do students go about writing their stories? Do they pick the situation or category first and then find things that would fit? Do any students start with the numbers?

- How do students determine the number of things in their stories? Do they seem to randomly pick numbers at first and then figure out what they need at the end? Do they use smaller or larger numbers?

- Are students able to write number sentences for their stories? Do they relate the numbers in their stories to the number sentences? Do they use conventional ways to write their number sentences, such as:

$$8 + 4 = 12 \qquad \text{or} \qquad \begin{array}{r} 8 \\ + 4 \\ \hline 12 \end{array}$$

- If students are having difficulty with number combinations, suggest that they get cubes to equal the number they are working with and show them how to break apart this set of cubes into groups. After they have made groups, encourage them to check their total number of cubes each time.

❖ **Tip for the Linguistically Diverse Classroom** Students with limited English proficiency can record their story using illustrations in a story board format. For example, using three pictures, students can illustrate the scene in the beginning of the story, the action that takes place, and how the story ends. Students might add a word below each picture to help describe what is taking place. A number sentence that describes the story can be written on the other side of the paper.

When students have finished, organize them into groups of four. Each student reads his or her story to the group and shares the number sentence and category. The group decides if they agree with the number sentence.

Collect the stories and put them together in a book. Ask volunteers to make a cover and title page for the book.

Session 8 Follow-Up

Ways to Get to _____ Students make their own miniversion of *12 Ways to Get to 11*. Choose a number or have students choose a number. For homework, they write three or four story problems that represent their number on Student Sheet 10, Ways to Get to _____. Remind them that their stories should focus on a specific category of items.

 **Homework**

Geometric Counts

What Happens

Sessions 1 and 2: Geoblock Faces and Pattern Block Puzzles Students identify Geoblocks by matching faces of a block to outlines on task cards. They find and record many different ways to fill outlines of various shapes with pattern blocks. They are introduced to *Shapes* software and a computer choice.

Sessions 3 and 4: Counting Geoblocks and Pattern Blocks Students count the number of different Geoblocks and record that number on a card to be shared during Session 6. They cover shapes with different arrangements of pattern blocks and record the numbers of blocks used.

Session 5: Sorting Geoblocks Students sort Geoblocks based on attributes they identify. They are introduced to a new choice, Mystery Block.

Session 6: Pattern Block Counts Students find the greatest, fewest, and other numbers of blocks that will cover pattern block shapes. They are introduced to a new computer choice. Near the end of the session, they open the Geoblock Count Box and compare their counts of the number of different Geoblocks.

Mathematical Emphasis

- Exploring and describing two-dimensional geometric shapes
- Exploring, sorting, and describing three-dimensional geometric shapes
- Finding different shapes and arrangements to cover patterns
- Finding and recording several solutions to a problem

I counted 18 different Geoblocks

I contD21 diffrenT geoblKs

What to Plan Ahead of Time

Materials

- Pattern blocks: 1 bucket per 6–8 students (Sessions 1–6)
- Geoblocks: 2 sets, divide each set into 2 or 3 subsets (Sessions 1–6)
- Overhead projector (Sessions 1–4, 6)
- Resealable plastic bags or envelopes: about 3 (Sessions 1–2)
- Paper or cloth bags: 3 or 4 (Session 5)
- Index cards: 1 per student (Sessions 3–5)
- Stick-on notes: several (Session 5)
- Computers: Macintosh II or above, with 4 MB of internal memory (RAM) and Apple System Software 7.0 or later: 1 for every 4–6 students (all sessions, optional)
- Apple Macintosh disk, *Shapes* (all sessions, optional)
- A projector or large-screen monitor for whole-class viewing (Session 6, optional)
- Paper, 12" by 18" (several sheets) and 8½" by 11" (1 sheet) plus chart paper (Session 5)

Other Preparation

- Duplicate the following student sheets and teaching resources (located at the end of this unit) in the following quantities. If you have Student Activity Booklets, copy only the transparencies marked with an asterisk.

For Sessions 1–2

Student Sheet 11, Ways to Fill—Pattern 1 (p. 194) and Student 12, Ways to Fill—Pattern 2 (p. 195): 1 per student, and a transparency of Student Sheet 11*

Find the Block Task Cards (p. 202): 3 sets. The cards will last longer if duplicated on heavy paper. Sets can be stored in envelopes or resealable plastic bags.

For Sessions 3–4

Student Sheet 13, Cover and Count (Shapes A–B) (p. 196), Student Sheet 14, Cover and Count (Shapes C–D) (p. 197), and Student Sheet 15, Cover and Count (Shapes E–F) (p. 198): 1 per student

Student Sheet 16, Cover and Count Recording Sheet (p. 199): 2–3 per student, and a transparency* (This will be used again in Session 6.)

Student Sheet 17, Tomorrow's Number (p. 200): 1 per student (homework)

For Session 6

Student Sheet 13, Cover and Count (Shapes A–B) (p. 196): transparency*

Student Sheet 18, Finding Shapes (p. 201): 1 per student (homework)

- Separate each tub of Geoblocks into two or three equal sets. (Sessions 1–2)
- Do the pattern blocks and Geoblocks activities yourself before introducing them to students. This helps you anticipate difficulties and provides insights for observing students. (Sessions 1–2)
- If you are using computers with this unit, install *Shapes* on each available computer. Read the *Shapes* Teacher Tutorial (p. 135) and try the activities. If you have fewer than the recommended computers, see the **Teacher Note**, Managing the Computer Activities (p. 61).
- Make a Geoblock Count Box. This can be as simple as a small cardboard box with a lid. (The box should be big enough to hold 30 index cards.) Cover the box and cut a slot on the top for students to drop in cards. (Sessions 3–4)

Geoblock Faces and Pattern Block Puzzles

Materials

- Computers with *Shapes* software installed (optional)
- Pattern blocks (1 bucket per 6–8 students)
- Prepared sets of Geoblocks
- Prepared sets of Find the Block Task Cards (3 sets)
- Student Sheets 11 and 12 (1 per student)
- Transparency of Student Sheet 11
- Overhead projector
- Resealable plastic bags or envelopes

What Happens

Students identify Geoblocks by matching faces of a block to outlines on task cards. They find and record many different ways to fill outlines of various shapes with pattern blocks. They are introduced to *Shapes* software and a computer choice. Their work focuses on:

- identifying geometric terms for different shapes
- covering designs in many different ways
- counting faces of Geoblocks
- identifying a Geoblock by looking at its faces
- devising ways to record their work

Start-Up

Today's Number   Students brainstorm ways to express the number of days they have been in school. You might suggest that students use combinations of 10 to start their equations. Add a card to the class counting strip and fill in another number on the blank 200 chart. For full directions on this activity, see p. 124.

On-Computer Activity: Introducing *Shapes* Software

The use of computer activities is optional in this unit. However, if you have computers available, it is recommended that you use the software. The computer work is integrated into the units and enriches the work students do. Many of the computer activities have no counterparts when using the manipulative materials.

The purpose for using *Shapes* in this unit is similar to the purpose for using manipulatives. Students will become familiar with the software—explore the program, see how it works, and learn how to use the tools specific to the program. Although the computer choice is included only in this investigation of the introductory unit, you may continue the choice in later investigations and units. It is particularly important that students have frequent opportunities to use computers and *Shapes* if you are planning to do the Geometry and Fractions unit later in the year.

Note: Before showing students how to use *Shapes*, use the *Shapes* tutorial (p. 135) and try the activities yourself on the computer.

Gather the students around the largest computer display you have to introduce the program. If your display is small, you may want to introduce the software to smaller groups over several days. Tell them that they will build pictures and designs with *Shapes* just like they do with pattern blocks. Demonstrate the following on the computer:

- How to open *Shapes* by double-clicking on the icon.
- How to select an activity (for example, Free Explore) by clicking on it once.
- How to read the directions, then click on [OK], or press the <return> key.
- How to get several shapes from the *Shapes* window.
- How to slide shapes by dragging them (point out that they snap into position when their sides are close).
- How to turn shapes with the two Turn tools.
- How to use the Erase One tool to erase one shape at a time and the Erase All button to erase all the shapes.

Tell students that they will use all these tools to make their own designs.

See the **Teacher Note**, Managing the Computer Activities (p. 61), for suggestions on how to structure the computer choice depending on the number of computers you have available.

Activity

Find the Block

If students have had frequent opportunities to explore pattern blocks and Geoblocks since they were introduced in Investigation 1, they will be more ready to do the specific tasks in this investigation. If students have explored the materials during only one or two math sessions, you may want to provide time for them to use the materials at other times during the day. In this investigation, students will be using pattern blocks and Geoblocks as they try geometric activities.

For the next few weeks, we are going to be working on *geometry*. Does anyone have an idea about the kinds of activities we might be doing?

Sometimes we will be working with flat or two-dimensional shapes like the pattern blocks. Other times we will be using solid or three-dimensional shapes, like Geoblocks.

Pass around a set of Geoblocks and have each student take out one block. Discuss what the word *face* means and give examples of different meanings. Introduce the geometric meaning of *face*.

Another meaning of *face* is a side of a block. When you put your block down on the floor or a table, it sits on one of its *faces*. When you touch a face of a block with the palm of your hand, it feels flat and smooth. What shapes are some of the faces on your block?

Count the sides, or faces, on your block. How many faces does it have?

Record the different numbers on the board. Then sort the blocks by the number of faces, asking students whose blocks have the same number of faces to stand together.

Ask students to look at other blocks in the group they are standing with to make sure they all have the same number of faces. Then return the blocks to the tub or container.

Introduce the Choice Time activity by showing students the set of Find the Block Task Cards. Using one card and a block as a model, explain that the shapes on the card match all the faces of *one* block. Students are to find the block that matches each card. Students find a block for a task card, then trade cards with partners and find the block for the other card. Partners compare their blocks to see if they agree.

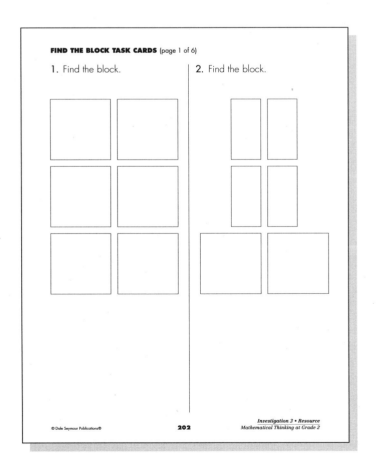

Ways to Fill

Filling with One Shape Distribute a set or bag of pattern blocks to each table or group and a copy of Student Sheet 11, Ways to Fill—Pattern 1, to each student. Place a transparency of the student sheet on the overhead.

Look at the outline at the top of the page. Fill it in using one pattern block shape. For example, try to fill it using only triangles, only squares, or only trapezoids. When you have filled it using only one shape block, record how you filled it in on the space labeled "1 Shape."

Encourage students to record their response using any recording method that makes sense to them. When they have filled the outline using one shape, students slide the blocks onto their desk to save them and fill the outline again using a different-shaped block.

Ask students to try filling in the outline several ways using only one shape and to record each way they find. Let students share their findings with the whole class. On the board, record students' various ways of recording. Some students may have drawn pictures of the blocks; others may have used numbers and words, such as "2 hexagons." Others may have used abbreviations such as 6 T (for 6 triangles), 6 G (for 6 green), or 6 Δs.

Two yellow or two hexagons is one way. Who found this way to cover the shape? How did you record this? [*Write students' responses on the board.*] **Did anyone fill the outline in a different way?**

Students can share their ways until all four ways of filling the outline have been identified. Then ask students whether anyone has found another way. Rather than telling them that all the ways to fill the shape have been identified, you can promote their thinking by encouraging and expecting them to tell you when all ways have been found. Some students may suggest solutions that use blocks in two or more shapes. Remind them that, for now, they're trying to fill the outline with just one shape at a time.

You all agree that we can fill the outline only four ways using blocks of only one shape: two yellow hexagons, four red trapezoids, six blue rhombuses, or twelve green triangles. Was anyone able to fill the outline using orange squares or thin white rhombuses? Why not?

Most students will give a comment such as, "They don't fit." Some students may believe that they just haven't found the way to do it yet. Tell students they may work on this problem during Choice Time.

Filling with Two Shapes Now ask students to fill the outline using two different shapes. They record each way they filled the outline in on the corresponding space on the student sheet. If students are unsure about how to record, suggest they choose one method from the board.

There seem to be a lot of ways to fill this space using two different shapes. I wonder how many different ways there are. You will have time to find out and also to try to fill it with three shapes and four shapes during Choice Time.

Choice Time

Post a list of the choices in the classroom. You may want to include the material needed in parentheses. Although Shapes Pictures is included as a Choice Time activity, your computer setup may require some accommodations. See the **Teacher Note**, Managing the Computer Activities, p. 61, for suggestions on how to structure the computer choice depending on the number of computers you have available. If you are not using computers, omit Choice 1.

---

1. Shapes Pictures (computer)

2. Find the Block

3. Ways to Fill

Remind students they should record the choices they do each day on their Weekly Log and that they are to place all completed student sheets and other work in their folders as they finish.

If you have divided the tub of Geoblocks into three sets, there should be enough for three groups of three to four students to use them at one time. You may want to identify three work areas that are not too close together so the sets don't get mixed.

Choice 1: Shapes Pictures

Materials: Computers with *Shapes* installed

Students use the Shapes Pictures activity in the *Shapes* software to make their own pictures or designs. If you wish to discuss students' work later, have them save their pictures on disk (see pp. 163 and 171). Students might also informally walk around to view each other's work.

Choice 2: Find the Block

Materials: Geoblocks; Find the Block Task Cards

Students find the Geoblock that matches all the face outlines on the task card. They leave the block with the task card for the teacher to check.

Choice 3: Ways to Fill

Materials: Student Sheets 11–12, Ways to Fill

Students cover the pattern on the student sheet with pattern blocks. They find all the ways using only blocks that are the same shape (for example, using only trapezoids or only triangles) and record the numbers of blocks it took for each shape. Then they find ways to cover the pattern using two different shapes, three different shapes, and four different shapes.

Observing the Students

In this investigation, all Choice Time activities are related to exploring and describing attributes of two- and three-dimensional shapes. Students use this information to sort shapes, to make shapes from other shapes, and to find several different combinations of shapes that fill the same design. Some things you might observe in the choice activities include the following.

Shapes Pictures

As you observe students, ask them to describe what they are doing. Talk to the students about the way they are moving the blocks (sliding the blocks, and using the Turn and possibly the Flip tools). This will help them become more aware of these geometric motions. Just as important, it will help them become familiar with seeing shapes in different orientations and realizing that changing the orientation does not affect the shape's name (class) or attributes.

If students indicate the need for them, introduce these tools:

- The Flip tools flip, or reflect, shapes over a vertical or horizontal line. If you click on the shape with the first Flip tool, the shape flips over a vertical line through the center of the shape.
- The Duplicate tool makes copies of shapes.
- The Arrow tool selects shapes. This is useful if students wish to apply a tool or command such as **Duplicate** or **Bring to Front** to several shapes at the same time.
- The Magnification tools allow you to make shapes bigger or smaller. *Shapes that are different sizes will not snap to each other.*

- The Glue tool glues several shapes together into a "group," a new composite shape that can be slid, turned, and flipped as a unit.
- The Hammer breaks apart a glued group with one click.

Find the Block

- Can students relate individual faces of a block to a whole block?
- Are students able to match single faces of a block to an outline?
- Can students identify the block where all faces match the outlines?
- Do partners agree on the block that matches a specific task card? If not, how do they resolve their differences?

Ways to Fill

- Are students seeing any relationships among the different shapes? For example, do they see that they can replace one hexagon with two trapezoids or with a trapezoid and three triangles?
- Do students see that some shapes (square and thin rhombus) won't fit on the patterns no matter how they are arranged?
- Do students have a recording method that is easy to understand?

Near the End of the Session Tell students when five or ten minutes remain in each session so they can finish and record their work. Review cleanup procedures, including how to return materials to storage areas and how to check the floor for stray blocks. Remind students to put their work in their folders and write in their Weekly Logs if they have not already done so.

Sessions 1 and 2 Follow-Up

 **Homework**

More Card Games at Home Students play the card games Tens Go Fish and Turn Over 10 at home with their families.

 **Extension**

Pattern Block Designs Have students use pattern blocks to build a design near a computer or on a transportable flat surface, and then copy the design onto the computer using the Shapes Pictures activity.

Managing the Computer Activities

The grade 2 *Investigations* curriculum uses two software programs developed especially for the curriculum. *Shapes* is introduced in *Mathematical Thinking at Grade 2* and used in *Shapes, Halves, and Symmetry*. *Geo-Logo* is introduced in *How Long? How Far?* Although the software is included in only these units, we recommend that students use the programs throughout the year. As students use the activities again and again, they develop skills and insights into important mathematical ideas.

How you use the computer activities in your classroom will depend on the number of computers you have available. Although we have included Free Explore in Choice Time activities, your computer setup may not be realistic for student use of computers during math class. If you have a computer lab available once a week or if you have only one or two computers in your classroom, you may want to schedule student use of computers throughout the day.

Regardless of the number of computers you can use, let students work in pairs on the computer. Working in pairs not only maximizes computer resources but also encourages students to consult, monitor, and teach one another. Generally, more than two students at one computer is difficult to manage; in most such cases, one or several students will end up having limited experience with the machine and the activity. But if you have an odd number of students, you can form one threesome.

Computer Lab If you have a computer laboratory that has one computer for each pair of students, let all students do the computer activities at the same time. During Choice Time, students will be able to work on other choices. Plan to have students use the computer lab for one or two periods a week.

Three to Six Computers The curriculum is written for this case, and in many ways it is the simplest to coordinate. If you have several computers in your classroom, you can use computer activities as a Choice Time activity. You might introduce use of the computer and software to the whole class, using a large-screen monitor or projection device, or to small groups gathered around a machine. Then pairs of students can cycle through the computers, just as they cycle through other choices. Each pair should spend at least 15 to 20 minutes at the computer in one session. It is important that every student get a chance to use the computers, so you may have to allow students to use the computers at other times of the day. Monitor computer use carefully to ensure access for all students.

One or Two Computers If you have only one or two computers in your classroom, students will need to use the computers throughout the school day so that every pair of students has sufficient opportunity to do the computer activities.

Many students who are using computers and the *Shapes* or *Geo-Logo* software for the first time will need assistance. Many of their questions will require only short answers or demonstrations. (See the Teacher Tutorial on p. 135.) You do not have to be the only source of help for these students. Often students who are more familiar with computers can assist those who need help. Encourage students to experiment and see if they can figure out what they need to do, and then to share what they've discovered with each other and with you. It is not unusual for students to discover things about the software that the teacher doesn't know.

Saving Student Work Students can save their work on the computer in two ways: on the computer's internal drive or on a disk. Instructions for saving work are on pp. 163 and 171 of the *Shapes* Teacher Tutorial.

Geoblocks are a set of wooden three-dimensional blocks. The blocks look similar to kindergarten blocks, but they are smaller and are related by volume. There are also several different sizes for many of the shapes. For example the set includes cubes in these sizes: 1-by-1, 2-by-2, and 3-by-3.

Most second graders love to build with these blocks—towers, towns, roads, ramps, bridges, and many other things. As with other manipulative materials, such as pattern blocks, most students will need time to explore the Geoblocks before they are ready to use them in more specified ways. During this informal building time, they intuitively learn many of the characteristics of the blocks. They may discover, for example, that they need to substitute two smaller blocks to use in their road when the larger blocks run out.

In real-life situations, we frequently use two-dimensional drawings to help us picture and represent three-dimensional things. For example, a blueprint provides instructions for building a house, a pattern for cutting out and sewing a

shirt, and a diagram for assembling a bike. One reason Geoblocks are included in the second grade materials is to provide students with the opportunity to work with three-dimensional materials and see the relationship between three- and two-dimensional shapes. (Although interlocking cubes are three-dimensional, their uniform size limits some of the relationships that can be explored.)

In this investigation, students examine Geoblocks and describe their attributes, sort the set, and find Geoblocks that match its two-dimensional faces. In addition, students count the number of different Geoblocks. The answer to how many different Geoblocks there are has not been provided. Students will come up with different counts for the set and should realize that more than one number can't be correct. This may challenge them to sort and count the set again. If students ask how many different blocks there are, you can honestly say, "I don't know." Give students the responsibility for finding out.

Identifying Pattern Blocks and Terminology   Teacher Note

The pattern block set is made up of six shapes: a hexagon, a trapezoid, a square, a triangle, and two parallelograms (rhombuses). In most sets, each shape comes in one color: the hexagons are yellow; the trapezoids are red, the squares are orange, the triangles are green, the narrow rhombuses are tan, and the wide rhombuses are blue.

Since all pattern blocks of the same color are the same shape, it is very natural for students to identify them by color. This is fine and should not be discouraged. At the same time, students should become familiar with and use correct geometric terms for different shapes. For pattern blocks, second grade students will easily identify the green block as a triangle and the orange block as a square. The terms *trapezoid* and *hexagon* may be new to many students. They will learn to use these words readily if you use them naturally and help them remember the words when they forget. To help students learn the names of the shapes, you may want to use the color along with the shape name for a while, such as yellow hexagons and red trapezoids.

How to identify the blue and tan blocks becomes a little more problematic since there is no unique term that applies to these blocks. Young children typically refer to them as diamonds. Along with the orange squares, they are rhombuses, and also they are parallelograms. This is because many geometric terms for shapes are part of a hierarchical classification system. For example, all squares are rectangles, but not all rectangles

are squares. The defining characteristics of four-sided shapes are:

> Square: 4 equal sides and 4 right angles
> Rhombus: 4 equal sides
> Rectangle: 4 right angles
> Parallelogram: 2 pairs of parallel sides
> Trapezoid: 4 sides and *only* two sides parallel
> Quadrilateral: 4 sides

The blue and tan blocks are identified as rhombuses. (The tan block is identified as the thin rhombus.) When you talk about these shapes, frequently use the term *parallelograms* so students become familiar with both terms. Identifying the blue block as a rhombus and the tan block as a parallelogram may lead to misconceptions about the differences between the two blocks. Students will still need to distinguish among the different blocks that are rhombuses, parallelograms, or diamonds.

Model the correct use of geometric terms but do not insist that students use them. As long as they are communicating effectively, let them use the language they are comfortable with, while you continue to model the correct language. You should be cautious while using the pattern blocks that you don't inadvertently lead students to misconceptions. For example, if a student says, "None of the blocks are rectangles," you might respond, "None of the blocks look like many of the rectangles you have seen. However, a square is a special kind of rectangle."

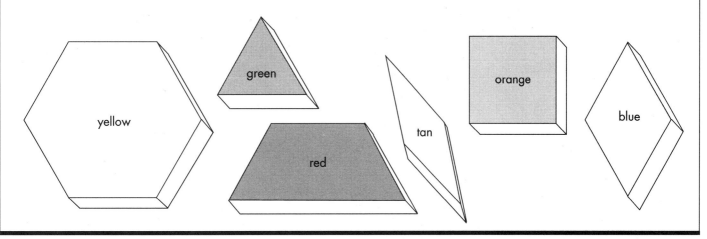

Counting Geoblocks and Pattern Blocks

Materials

- Pattern blocks (1 bucket per 6–8 students)
- Prepared sets of Geoblocks
- Index cards (1 per student)
- Geoblock Count Box
- Student Sheets 13–15 (1 per student)
- Student Sheet 16 (2–3 per student)
- Transparency of Student Sheet 16
- Overhead projector
- Computers with *Shapes* software installed (optional)
- Student Sheet 17 (1 per student, homework)

What Happens

Students count the number of different Geoblocks and record that number on a card to be shared during Session 6. They cover shapes with different arrangements of pattern blocks and record the numbers of blocks used. Their work focuses on:

- covering designs in many different ways
- sorting Geoblocks
- identifying a Geoblock by matching its faces to their outlines

Start-Up

Today's Number   Sometime during the school day, students brainstorm ways to express the number of days they have been in school. If students have been using combinations of 10 to start their equations in the last couple of sessions, you might have them discuss whether the order of the addends matters. For example, if Today's Number is 16, and a student has written
3 + 7 + 6 to show a combination of 10 plus 6 more, ask whether they still can see the 10 plus 6 if you rearrange the numbers to 3 + 6 + 7. For full directions on this routine, see p. 124.

Activity

How Many Different Geoblocks?

Pull out a couple of random Geoblocks from a set, and ask students to guess how many different Geoblocks there are.

You all have used the Geoblocks during the first investigation or the last two sessions. How many different Geoblocks do you think are in a set?

Accept guesses and ask students to explain how they made their guesses. You may want to discuss what makes blocks different from one another— blocks that are the same have the same shape and size, blocks that are the same shape but vary in size are different.

Tell students that one choice during Choice Time will be to count the Geoblocks. They will work with a partner or a small group and sort the blocks to find how many different Geoblocks there are.

Hold up an index card and the Geoblock Count Box. Write on the board:

I counted _____ different Geoblocks.

When your group has found out how many different Geoblocks there are, copy this sentence on a card and fill in the number of blocks you counted. Also put your names on the card. If people in your group disagree about the count, you may each complete your own card. Put the card in this Geoblock Count Box. Keep your count a secret. We will compare the counts when everybody has had a chance to count the blocks.

Place the Geoblock Count Box and the cards in a special place, perhaps on your desk.

Activity

Cover and Count

Introduce the new pattern block choice. Explain that this choice is very similar to Ways to Fill, but in this activity, students cover six different shapes, lettered A–F (Student Sheets 13–15), and record their solutions on a recording sheet. Display a transparency of Student Sheet 16, Cover and Count Recording Sheet, on the overhead and demonstrate how to record the number of blocks used. Students are to find as many different ways as possible to cover each recording sheet for each task card they do. Some students may fill more than one recording sheet for a shape.

Have students cover Shape A on Student Sheet 13 and record different ways on Student Sheet 16. Explain that later (in Session 6) they will be sharing their results.

Activity

Choice Time

Add the new Choices to the posted list when you introduce them.

> 1. Shapes Pictures (computer)
>
> 2. Find the Block (Geoblocks)
>
> 3. Ways to Fill (pattern blocks)
>
> **4. How Many Different Geoblocks?**
>
> **5. Cover and Count (pattern blocks)**

For the remainder of Sessions 3 and 4, students work on Choice Time activities. This will be the final chance for students to do the Ways to Fill choice. If they have not completed it, they should do so. Students who are working at How Many Different Geoblocks? should work together, since there are many different blocks and some distinctions between blocks are subtle.

You may want to specify how much students need to do before moving on to a new choice. For example, when they do Cover and Count, you may want students to find and record at least three ways to cover three of the shapes on the student sheets and for each student to find at least three of the Geoblocks that match Find the Block Task Cards. They should note on their Weekly Log which task cards they have completed.

You also might have students check with you before moving on to a new choice or at the end of each session. That will help you get a sense of what everyone is doing, especially students whom you haven't had an opportunity to observe during Choice Time. Also, it might help students to get started on choices the following day.

For a review of the descriptions of Choice 1: Shapes Pictures, Choice 2: Find the Block, and Choice 3: Ways to Fill, see p. 58.

Choice 4: How Many Different Geoblocks?

Materials: Geoblocks, index cards, Geoblock Count Box

Students count the number of different Geoblocks, write the number and their names on a card, and deposit the card in the Geoblock Count Box. They do not share their count with others until after the box is opened in Session 6. Students who work on this choice should not have to share a set of Geoblocks with students who are working on a different Geoblock choice.

Choice 5: Cover and Count

Materials: Pattern blocks; Student Sheets 13–15, Cover and Count; Student Sheet 16, Cover and Count Recording Sheet

Students cover a shape with pattern blocks and write how many blocks it took on their recording sheet. They then cover the shape with different blocks and record. They find several different ways of covering each shape. All students should do Shape A, since it will be used in Session 6.

Observing the Students

Some things you might observe in the new Choice Time activities include the following.

How Many Different Geoblocks?

To be done most efficiently, this activity requires that group members work together to sort the blocks. However, many students will start working on the task independently. If they do, you can learn a lot about students by not immediately intervening. Observe them as they approach and try to complete the task.

- Do the students realize that they need to see all the blocks in the set, including the ones others in their group are counting? Let the students resolve this problem. If students continue to work independently, you might then say to them, "Have you looked at all the blocks in the set? What about those that are being counted by another group?"
- Are students organizing and keeping track of the blocks? Are they sorting the blocks by overall shape, putting all the cubes together, or are they looking at each block individually?

Cover and Count

You may need to provide some students with assistance in completing the recording sheet.

- How do students find the total number of blocks for each covering? Do they record the number for each shape and then physically count the total number of blocks on the student sheet? Or do they add (or count) the numbers across the row on the recording sheet?
- Do students use relationships among the blocks when covering a shape a second or third time? Do they brush off the blocks after covering a shape and then randomly begin placing blocks again on the shape? Or are they more purposeful when creating their next covering, perhaps by replacing a hexagon with two trapezoids?

Sessions 3 and 4 Follow-Up

Tomorrow's Number Students record tomorrow's number five different ways on Student Sheet 17, Tomorrow's Number. If they wish, they can ask a family member to suggest a sixth way.

 **Homework**

Sorting Geoblocks

Materials

- Geoblocks, separated into three sets
- Large paper, 12"-by-18" (2 sheets)
- Small paper, 8½"-by-11" (1 sheet)
- Stick-on notes
- Paper or cloth bags (3 or 4)
- Additional choice materials (computer with *Shapes* software installed, pattern blocks)
- Chart paper

What Happens

Students sort Geoblocks based on attributes they identify. They are introduced to a new choice, Mystery Block. Their work focuses on:

- describing attributes of the Geoblocks
- sorting the blocks by attributes
- identifying a Geoblock by feel

Start-Up

Today's Number   Collect or post the homework students did showing five ways to write Today's Number. If some students got an additional way from a family member, have them share some of those ways. Complete directions for this routine begin on p. 124.

Activity

Teacher Checkpoint

Sorting Geoblocks

Call the class together in a circle. Pass a set of Geoblocks around and have each student take one block.

Look at your block. Describe your block to the person sitting next to you, then listen while your partner tells you about his or her block. How are your blocks alike? How are they different?

Provide time for students to describe their blocks. Then call the class together. Ask one student to stand, hold up his or her block, and describe one attribute of the block. Other students hold up their blocks if the statement is also true for their blocks.

Jeffrey, tell us one thing about your block. Now, everyone else look at your block. Is the statement Jeffrey made about his block also true for your block? If so, hold up your block.

Students may describe their blocks in imprecise ways. Common statements from second graders include: "My block is smooth," "My block is pointy," and "My block is a square." Students at this age have not developed much vocabulary for describing three-dimensional geometric shapes. The purpose of this activity is for students to begin to examine the blocks and look at different attributes of the set, rather than to focus on teaching students correct terminology. Students will begin to use the correct terminology over a long period of time as they use shapes and see a need for more precise language.

❖ **Tip for the Linguistically Diverse Classroom**   Suggest that students with a limited English proficiency describe an attribute of their block non-verbally. For example, a student might outline the shape of the block with his or her finger to indicate a square or a rectangle. Or a student might hold up the number of fingers that corresponds to the number of sides on the block.

Place one small and two large sheets of paper in the center of the circle. Label the large sheets Match and Don't Match.

I would like a volunteer to put his or her block on the small paper, then tell us one thing that you notice about your block.

If necessary, ask the student to clarify the description. On a stick-on note write the word that describes the attribute and place it on the small paper next to the block.

The rest of the students determine whether the statement also applies to their blocks, then place their blocks on either the Match or Don't Match paper. Students examine both sets to see if blocks are correctly placed. Then they take back their blocks.

Try this several times with different students offering attributes that describe their blocks. Notice the attributes students suggest. Do students suggest geometric attributes, such as number of sides or shape of faces, or do they focus on attributes such as made of wood? Do students suggest attributes that differentiate the blocks? There will be times, however, when everyone's block matches the attribute, for example, "My block has cor-ners" or "My block is smooth."

At the end of the activity, attach the notes to chart paper to begin a list of descriptive words. More attributes can be added as students continue to use Geoblocks.

Choice Time

Introduce the new choice, Mystery Block. In this partner activity, one student secretly places a Geoblock in a bag. The other student tries to find an identical block by reaching in the bag and feeling the secret block. Ask two volunteers to demonstrate the activity.

Add Mystery Block to the posted list and cross off Ways to Fill. If all students have had an opportunity to complete Find the Block, you may want to also cross off that choice.

---

1. Shapes Pictures (Computer)

2. Find the Block

3. ~~Ways to Fill (pattern blocks)~~

4. How Many Different Geoblocks?

5. Cover and Count

6. **Mystery Block**

For the remainder of Session 5, students work on choices. Students who are using Geoblocks can share sets if they are doing Find the Block and/or Mystery Block.

You may find that at the end of this investigation many students will want to continue working on these choices. Consider having math materials available for students to use during times when they have free choices. Students benefit from many repeated experiences with a material over a long period of time.

Descriptions of Choice 1: Shapes Pictures and Choice 2: Find the Blocks, begin on p. 58; Choice 4: How Many Different Geoblocks? and Choice 5: Cover and Count reviews begin on p. 66.

Choice 6: Mystery Block

Materials: Geoblocks, bags

Students work with a partner and take turns hiding or identifying a mystery block. While the partner's back is turned, the student chooses a block and puts it in a bag. Then the partner reaches in the bag without looking, feels the block, and finds an identical block in the set.

Observing the Students

The following questions provide some observation guidelines for you to use as you watch students at the Mystery Block activity. Refer to previous sessions for observation suggestions for the other choices.

Mystery Block

- Are students able to find a matching block without using their eyes?
- Do they need to confirm their match by looking at the blocks? Does this seem easy or difficult?

Pattern Block Counts

What Happens

Students find the greatest, fewest, and other numbers of blocks that will cover pattern block shapes. They are introduced to a new computer choice. Near the end of the session, they open the Geoblock Count Box and compare their counts of the number of different Geoblocks. Their work focuses on:

- finding the greatest and fewest pattern blocks that will cover the same shape
- finding and describing equivalent ways to cover a design
- comparing counts and discussing why counts of the same thing don't agree

Start-Up

Today's Number Sometime during the school day, students brainstorm ways to express the number of days they have been in school. If students haven't included subtraction in their ways to express Today's Number, you might suggest that they try to do so. Add a card to the class counting strip and fill in another number on the blank 200 chart. See p. 124 for full directions on this routine.

Materials

- Pattern blocks
- Student work from Sessions 3 and 4, Student Sheets 13–16
- Geoblock Count Box
- Transparency of Student Sheet 13
- Transparency of Student Sheet 16 (optional)
- Overhead projector
- Computers with *Shapes* software installed (optional)
- Student Sheet 18 (1 per student, homework)
- Large-screen monitor (optional)

Activity

Cover and Count: How Many Blocks?

Today we're going to investigate the different number of blocks that can cover some of the Cover and Count shapes. Take out your Cover and Count Student Sheets and your Recording Sheet.

Distribute pattern blocks. Display a transparency of Shape A on the overhead.

Who thinks he or she used the *greatest* total number of blocks to cover Shape A? How many blocks did you use?

Record the numbers students offer on the chalkboard. Ask students to name the greatest number recorded, then ask the class to try to cover their designs with this number of blocks. Then they share with the class how they covered the design.

What is the fewest number of blocks that will cover Shape A?

If students insist that five is the fewest number of blocks, challenge them to find a way to cover it using only four blocks. (Shape A can be covered with 4, 5, 6, 7, 8, 9, or 10 pattern blocks.)

Is there more than one way to cover Shape A with exactly six blocks? What ways did you find?

Record students' results on a transparency of Student Sheet 16, Cover and Count Recording Sheet, or on the board. Have students test each way by trying to fill Shape A with the specified number of blocks.

Have students pick one or two other Cover and Count shapes, investigate ways to cover them, then share their results.

- **What is the fewest number of blocks that will cover the shape?**
- **What is the greatest number of blocks that will cover the shape?**
- **Can we cover the shape with all the numbers between the fewest and greatest?**

If you are not introducing the new computer choice, students can investigate the different number of blocks that will cover other Cover and Count shapes or work on Choice Time activities for the remainder of the session.

Activity

On-Computer Activity: Solve *Shapes* Puzzles

If all students have had an opportunity to use the computer at least once, introduce a new computer choice, Solve Puzzles found on the *Shapes* software. The use of this activity is optional. However, if available, it is recommended that you use the software. In this activity, which is similar to Cover and Count, students fill in outlines that the software places on the screen. Plan to continue using this activity and the other computer activity, Shapes Pictures, as choices for the remainder of the unit.

You may want to introduce the new computer activity to small groups of students or to the entire class if you have a large-screen display. Gather students around the screen and open the *Shapes* software. Choose the Solve Puzzles activity by clicking on it once. Read the directions, then click on [OK] or press <return>. Outline Number 1 appears. Students' task is to cover the outline using shapes from the shape bar.

If you wish to discuss students' work later, they can save their solutions on disk by clicking **File, Save My Work** from the menu bar at the top of the screen.

For a written record of students' work, they can select **Windows**, **Show Notes** from the menu. Students can record their notes, then select **Print** for a written record of their work.

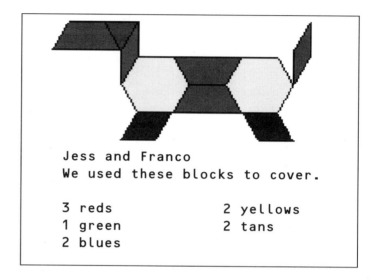

Jess and Franco
We used these blocks to cover.

3 reds
1 green
2 blues

2 yellows
2 tans

Choose **Number 6** from the **Number** menu. Tell students that their challenge on puzzles 5 to 10 is to fill the outlines with the *fewest* blocks possible.

You may wish to ask a student to demonstrate moving several shapes onto an outline of one of the shapes before closing the activity. Determine whether there is time to do any Choice Time activities during this session or whether the new computer activity should begin during Investigation 4.

Observing the Students As students work, talk with them about the way they are sliding the blocks and using the Turn and Flip tools. This will help them become more aware of these geometric motions. Just as important, it will help them become familiar with seeing shapes in different orientations and realize that changing the orientation does not affect the shape's name or attributes.

The tasks are somewhat different for each of the outlines. Encourage students to compare their results.

Numbers 1 to 5 are interpretable pictures. They can be filled in several ways, and discussions of how one group could fill Number 1 with 10 shapes while another group filled it with 12 can be interesting.

Numbers 6 to 10 are simple shapes with larger internal areas that can be filled in several ways. Ask students how they could "prove" that they have filled each with the fewest blocks possible.

Opening the Geoblock Count Box

All students should have had at least one opportunity to do the How Many Different Geoblocks? choice. (If not, encourage students to do this choice within the next few days and include this activity during the next investigation.)

About 10 or 15 minutes before the session ends, tell students that today they are going to open the Geoblock Count Box and find out how many different blocks they counted. You may want to be dramatic!

Today is the day many of you have been waiting for! We're going to open the Geoblock Count Box and see how many blocks people counted. Do you think everybody counted the same number?

Remove the cards from the box one at a time, recording each number on the board. Have different students come up, take a card from the box, and read aloud the count. When the numbers on all the cards have been recorded on the board, ask the students what they think of the results. If all the students agree, the activity is over. However, in most second grade classrooms, students get a number of different counts. Instead of telling them which number is correct, ask students to verify the answers themselves. This will take time, perhaps most of the year, as students, by their own choice, return to the problem again and again. By letting students find the answer themselves, their interest will be sustained and they will remain engaged in the activity. You might make statements such as:

I wonder why we have so many different counts? I wonder which number is correct? I don't know how many different blocks there are. If you want to know, you'll have to find out yourselves. You can choose to do this activity again during Choice Time or free time in other units.

If students are interested and are keeping track of the results, you might post the cards or create a graph, grouping together all counts that are the same. Tell students that they can change their count at any time by removing their old card and replacing it with a new one.

Session 6 Follow-Up

Finding Shapes Students look for things around their homes or neighborhoods that have the same shape, or close to the same shape, as pattern blocks. They record what they find on Student Sheet 18, Finding Shapes.

 **Homework**

Counting

What Happens

Session 1: Enough for the Class? Students determine how many people are in their class. Working in pairs, they use this information to determine whether there are enough cubes in a bag for each person in the class to have one and how many leftovers there will be. Students write an explanation of the strategy they used to solve the problem.

Session 2: Counting Coins, Counting Choices Students are introduced to a counting game called Collect 25¢, which uses money. This game and the activities Enough for the Class? and Exploring Coins are choices for the rest of the session.

Sessions 3 and 4: Counting Strips and Counting Choices Students are introduced to counting strips. This activity, along with Collect 25¢, Exploring Coins, and Enough for the Class? are choices for the next two sessions.

Session 5: Enough for the Class? Revisited Students work on an Enough for the Class? problem that is used for assessment. They record their strategies for solving this problem and then discuss the problem as a class.

Mathematical Emphasis

- Counting 15–60 objects
- Counting by 2's, 5's, 10's, and other ways
- Comparing two sets by identifying how many more are needed or how many are extra
- Adding two-digit numbers
- Identifying coins and their values
- Combining coins to make 25¢ and 50¢

42 cubes in the bag.
29 kids in our class.
42 − 29 = 13
I counted up from 29
and got 13.
30, 31, 32, 33, 34, 35,
36, 37, 38, 39, 40, 41, 42.
13 cubes are extra.

42 cubes

What to Plan Ahead of Time

Materials

- Interlocking cubes (all sessions)
- Resealable plastic bags or envelopes: about 10–15 (Session 1)
- Countable objects such as pennies, buttons, cubes (Sessions 1, 5)
- Chart paper (Sessions 2, 5)
- Plastic coin sets (real coins may be substituted), 30 pennies, 20 nickels, 20 dimes: 1 set per 3–4 students (Sessions 2–4)
- Small cups or containers for storing coin sets: 1 per 3–4 students (Sessions 2–4)
- Number cubes with dots or numbers 1–6: 1 per group of 3–4 students (Sessions 2–4)
- Tape (Sessions 3–4)
- Adding-machine tape: 2 rolls (Sessions 3–4)

Other Preparation

- Duplicate the following student sheets and teaching resources (located at the end of this unit) in the following quantities. If you have Student Activity Booklets, copy only the extra materials marked with an asterisk.

For Session 1

Student Sheet 19, Enough for the Class? (p. 208): 1 per student, plus some extras*

For Session 2

Student Sheet 19, Enough for the Class? (p. 208): 1 per student

Student Sheet 20, Exploring Coins (p. 209): 1 per student (homework)

For Sessions 3–4

Student Sheet 21, Counting Strips (p. 210): 1 per student (homework)

For Session 5

Student Sheet 19, Enough for the Class? (p. 208): 1 per student

- Fill a resealable plastic bag with 11–13 more cubes than the number of students in the class, for class work. (Session 1)
- Prepare counting bags by filling 10–15 resealable plastic bags with various numbers (15–60) of objects, for class work. Letter each bag for identification. (Session 1. These bags will be used again in Sessions 2–4 during Choice Time activities.)
- Prepare sets of coins for each group of 3–4 students. Each set should contain 30 pennies, 20 nickels, and 20 dimes. Sets can be stored in small cups or containers. (Sessions 2–4)
- Cut adding-machine tape into strips about 2 feet long. Each student will need several strips. (Sessions 3–4)
- Fill a resealable plastic bag with two colors of cubes, for class work. The total amount should equal a few less than the number of students in the class. (Session 5)

Enough for the Class?

Materials

- Prepared bag with cubes, for class work
- Prepared counting bags for students (about 10–15)
- Interlocking cubes
- Student Sheet 19 (1 per student plus extras)

What Happens

Students determine how many people are in their class. Working in pairs, they use this information to determine whether there are enough cubes in a bag for each person in the class to have one and how many leftovers there will be. Students write an explanation of the strategy they used to solve the problem. Their work focuses on:

- counting a quantity in more than one way
- comparing two amounts
- writing about solutions using words and numbers

Start-Up

Today's Number   Sometime during the school day, students brainstorm ways to express the number of days they have been in school. They add a card to the class counting strip and fill in another number on the blank 200 chart. See p. 124 for full directions on this routine.

Activity

How Many People Are in Our Class?

The number of people in the class will be an important piece of information in the next activity and the final investigation when students play the game Guess My Rule. As a whole class, determine the total number of students in two ways: by adding the number of boys and the number of girls and by adding small clusters of students. If students are arranged in clusters of desks, use these numbers. If you have gathered students together in a meeting area, divide them into smaller groups (at least three groups) either by how they are sitting, by age, or by an attribute.

Today we are going to work on an activity that requires knowing how many students are in our class. As a group, we are going to figure this out in two different ways. One way is by adding the number of boys and girls together, and the other way is by adding the number of people at each table.

Record the following information on the board:

```
People sitting at          Number of students
each table                 in our class

Table 1: 6   Table 4: 5    Girls: 16
Table 2: 6   Table 5: 5    Boys: 16
Table 3: 5   Table 6: 5
```

The students may already know the total number of students in the class. This will not limit the activity, because once students determine the total by adding subgroups (boys plus girls), they can check their answer against the information they know.

Before you begin to work on this problem, think about whether we will get the same number of people if we add the boys and girls (16 + 16, for example) as when we add the number of people at each table (6 + 6 + 5 + 5 + 5 + 5).

Some second grade students will be certain that the two totals will be equal and offer an idea such as, "They both tell you how many people are in the class. No matter what combinations of numbers you add, they should equal the same amount." There will, however, be students who have not yet solidified their understanding of this idea and reach the wrong conclusion in much the same way as they might if you ask them if they would get a different total if they count a set of objects by 1's and then by 2's or 5's. These students will not necessarily see that the two problems that represent groups of students in the class should be equivalent.

Encourage all students to explain their thinking. Over time and with repeated experiences, students will develop an understanding of this idea.

For the next few minutes, I'd like you to talk to a partner about how you would solve these two problems. Remember, we are trying to find out how many students are in our classroom.

Since you will be solving these problems together as a whole group, it is not necessary that students have materials. After a few minutes, call the group together and ask students to share strategies for solving the two problems. Focus on one problem at a time. As students offer ideas, record them on the board, then choose one or two of the ways to solve each problem.

People sitting at each table		Number in class
Table 1: 6	Table 4: 5	Girls: 16 Boys: 16
Table 2: 6	Table 5: 5	
Table 3: 5	Table 6: 5	

- Use cubes and build a tower for each, then add them all up.
- Add 5 + 5 + 5 + 5, then add 6 + 6.
- Add 10 + 10 and 6 + 6. Add these together.

- Make two towers of 16 each.
- Use your fingers and count up from 16.
  17, 18, 19, 20, 21, 22, 23, 24, 25, 26, 27, 28, 29, 30, 31, 32.

Choose one or two methods, and as a class add up the number of boys and girls and the number of people sitting in clusters.

After the class has determined the total number of people, students may want to count off as a way of checking their work.

Activity

Enough for the Class?

Provide each student with Student Sheet 19, Enough for the Class? Hold up a bag that you have filled with 11–13 more cubes than the number of students in your class. Ask students if they think there are enough cubes in the bag for everyone in the class to have one. Ask for suggestions of how you might find out if there are enough for the class.

As a class, count the cubes in the bag. Ask for ideas about how to check this count, and use one of the strategies the students suggest to do so.

We've counted the cubes in the bag, and we know that there are enough for everyone to have one cube. If everyone takes one cube, how many cubes will be left in the bag? Work with partners and solve this problem. Then each of you should write about how you solved it on your student sheet.

Remind students that mathematicians write about how they solved problems so they can communicate their ideas to others. Suggest that students use words, numbers, and/or pictures to help explain their thinking. See the **Teacher Note**, Writing and Recording (p. 82), for suggestions about how to encourage and support students' writing in math class.

❖ **Tip for the Linguistically Diverse Classroom** Pair English-proficient students with second-language learners. Suggest that the student with limited proficiency draw a storyboard to show how he or she solved the problem, while the student proficient in English adds words to clarify the drawings.

As students are working, observe how they are solving the problems and also how they are organizing their written explanation. When students finish, ask them to read their explanation first to their partners and then to you. If any part of their explanation is unclear, or if they have left out a part, suggest that they go back and revise their work.

Students can then choose another bag of objects, count how many there are in the bag, determine if there are enough for the class, and figure out how many would be left over. They should record their work on a new copy of Student Sheet 19. Remind students to record the letter of the bag they worked with.

When most students have finished solving the initial problem, gather the class together and ask for volunteers to share their writing with the class. Suggest that students also share any pictures or diagrams they used as part of their solutions. There will probably be a variety of strategies and explanations as well as a variety of solutions. The **Dialogue Box**, Are There Enough for the Class? (p. 85), provides some examples of strategies used by students to determine how many leftovers there were in an Enough for the Class? problem.

As a class, count the leftovers in the bag. Some students may wish to revise their work. Encourage them to do so on the back of their paper.

Leave 5 minutes at the end of this session for students to fill out their Weekly Logs.

> *Writing and Recording*

Just as students should be engaged in frequent mathematical conversation, so too should they be encouraged to explain their problem-solving strategies in writing and with pictures and diagrams. Writing about how they solved a problem is a challenging task for young students. As with any writing assignment, many will need support and encouragement as they begin to find ways of communicating their ideas and thinking on paper.

The range of students' abilities to write and record varies greatly in any second grade classroom. In part this is because students are just beginning to feel comfortable in the areas of reading and writing, and in part because reflecting on one's own thinking is a challenging task. Initially, some students will record a few words and possibly some numbers that describe their strategy, while others might be able to write considerably more. Drawing pictures as part of their explanation is often a way into the task for many students. Explain to students that mathematicians often write and draw about their ideas as a way of explaining
to others how they are thinking. The more often students are encouraged (and expected) to write and record their ideas, the more comfortable and fluent they become.

Students benefit tremendously from discussing their ideas prior to writing about them. Sometimes this might happen in pairs, and other times it happens in large-group discussions. Questions and prompts such as "How did you solve the problem?" or "Can you tell me what you did after you put the cubes into groups of 5?" may help extend students' thinking. During whole-class discussion, it is important to model writing and recording strategies for students so that they can see how their mathematical strategies might get recorded using words, numbers, and/or pictures. For example, when Jeffrey reported to the class how he solved an Enough for the Class? problem, he said:

Jeffrey: I put the cubes in groups of 5, and then I counted 5, 10, 15, 20, 25, but there was 1 left over so that made 26.

His teacher recorded the strategy on the board. As she recorded, she reiterated his strategy in words:

> I counted by 5's—5, 10, 15, 20, 25.
> 25 + 1 = 26 cubes

By recording student explanations on the board, you begin to build up some possible models for them to use as they write about their thinking.

As with any type of writing, providing feedback to students is an important part of the process. As the audience for your students' work, you can point out those ideas that clearly convey student thinking and those that need more detail. Quite often by having students read their work aloud to you or to a peer, they themselves can identify ideas that are unclear and parts that are incomplete.

Continued on next page

The following are examples of the sort of responses you might expect from second graders early in the school year. The students were taking inventories of items in their classroom.

Camilla used pictures, numbers, and words in her explanation of how she counted the erasers in the classroom. She communicated the counting strategy simply and clearly. This could be one piece in a collection of work that would provide a record of how Camilla's counting strategies changed over time.

Temara organized the chess pieces into groups in order to count them, although it is unclear how she actually counted the pieces. A follow-up question for Temara might be, "Can you explain how you counted each group of chess pieces?"

Name _____ Camilla

Inventories

I inventoried _____ erasers _____.

This is how many there are ___ 23 ___.

This is how I counted them.

1 2 3 4 5 6 7 8 9 10 11 12 13 14
15 16 17 18 19 20 21 22 23

O O O O O O O O O O O
O O O O O O O O O O
O

I counted by: ones

Name _____ Temara

Inventories

I inventoried _____ chess peses _____.

This is how many there are ___ 24 ___.

This is how I counted them.

I contied by shaps and sises and colors

Continued on next page

Bjorn explained in words how he counted the books in the classroom. He went on to use number sentences to indicate how he added. The teacher might suggest to Bjorn that he use a complete sentence instead of just saying "by 5's." When Bjorn writes 10 + 10 = 20, 2 + 20 = 22, it appears that there were 2 books left over, which he added to the 20 to get 22. A follow-up comment for Bjorn might be to point out that this part of his explanation is unclear and to ask him what he could include to make the explanation clearer to others.

Harris made a list of the marbles that he inventoried. Although he doesn't say so in words, it is clear from his list that he first grouped the marbles according to color, counted the marbles in each group, and then added the groups together. Initially Harris's paper had only the list of numbers going down the left side, and the total of 59. When he shared his work, he was asked to explain how he added the list of numbers. Harris went back and added the subtotals to the right and underneath the column of numbers.

Name _____ Bjorn _____

Inventories

I inventoried _____ published books _____.

This is how many there are 22 _____.

This is how I counted them.

by 5's

$5 + 5 = 10 \quad 5 + 5 = 10$

$10 + 10 = 20 \quad 2 + 20 = 22$

Name _____ Harris _____

Inventories

I inventoried _____ MarBLS _____.

This is how many there are _____.

This is how I counted them.

8
$+$
$8 = 16$
$+$
$10 = 26$
$+$
$6 = 32$
$+$
$10 + 8 + 9 = 59$
$42 \quad 50 \quad 59$

8 GreeN
8 cLeR
10 BLACK
6 WiTE
10 ReD
8 Hello
9 BLUE

The examples shown represent early attempts by second grade students to communicate their counting strategies in words, numbers, and pictures. This first unit, *Mathematical Thinking,* is a place to introduce students to writing as a part of mathematics. As the year progresses, you may be surprised and impressed by the progress students have made in communicating their problem-solving strategies through writing.

Are There Enough for the Class?

After working on the Enough for the Class? problem (p. 80), these second grade students meet to share their strategies for finding how many cubes would be left over if each student took 1 cube from a bag with 38 cubes. There are 26 students in the class.

Before we talk about strategies, what did you get as an answer to this problem?

[*Many students respond with 12, but 10 and 64 also come up.*]

Lila: I got 64, but I know it couldn't be that.

What makes you think that the answer couldn't be 64?

Lila: Well, there were only 38 cubes in the bag to begin with. What did I do?

Think about it during our discussion and see if it helps you to figure it out. OK, who wants to share a strategy?

Ebony: I wrote a 26 on my paper, and then I made little lines for every number up to 38. And then I counted them and I got 12. [*Ebony shows her paper to the class.*]

Jeffrey: I just made 26 circles, and then underneath those I made more circles until I got up to 38. Then I counted the circles underneath.

Jeffrey's way is similar to Ebony's way in that they both counted up from 26.

Chen: Mine's different. I made a train of cubes. Then I counted 26 cubes and broke off the rest and I had 10 left. So I think there's 10 left over.

Simon: But 26 and 10 is 36. There's 38 cubes in the bag.

So what should Chen do?

Simon: I think he counted out only 36 cubes. He should add on 2 more so that he has 38 in all.

[*Chen snaps his two trains plus 2 extra cubes together, then at the teacher's suggestion, he recounts and breaks off 26 cubes. He smiles as he counts 12 cubes in the leftover train.*]

OK, any more strategies? Two more? Wow! Franco first and then Karina.

Franco: I got 12 because the difference between 30 and 20 is 10, and the difference between 8 and 6 is 2. So add 10 and 2 and that's 12.

Karina: I started with 26 and then counted until 38.

Did you use your fingers to keep track?

[*Karina nods shyly.*]

I think that's great. Don't feel shy about that. That was a smart thing to do. You can use fingers or cubes or whatever you need. Mathematicians use all sorts of things to get their answers.

[*The teacher walks over to Lila and asks if she has figured out what she did to get 64.*]

Lila: I still can't figure out what I did.

Let's look at your work together. Why don't you try the problem again and see if you get a more reasonable answer.

Name Franco   Date

Student Sheet 19

Enough for the Class?

Find how many things are in the bag.
Find a way to check your count.

Bag _____

There are __38__ things in the bag.

$$30 - 20 = 10$$
$$8 - 6 = 2 \qquad 10 + 2 = 12$$

Are there enough for the class? __yes__

How many leftovers will you have? __12__

Explain how you figured this out.
Use numbers, words, or pictures.

the diverence in between 26 and 38 is 12, I know Because the diverence in between 30 and 20 is 10 and the diverence in between 6 and 8 is 2
and 2 + 10 = 12

   208   *Investigation 4 • Session 1 Mathematical Thinking at Grade 2*

Counting Coins, Counting Choices

Materials

- Coin sets (1 set per 3–4 students; add extra pennies if necessary)
- Number cubes with dots or numbers 1–6 (1 per group)
- Chart paper
- Student Sheet 19 (1 per student)
- Prepared counting bags (10–15)
- Student Sheet 20 (1 per student, homework)

What Happens

Students are introduced to a counting game called Collect 25¢ that uses money. This game, Enough for the Class?, and Exploring Coins are choices for the rest of the session. Students' work focuses on:

- counting objects
- counting orally
- exploring coins and their values

Start-Up

Today's Number Sometime during the school day, students brainstorm ways to express the number of days they have been in school. They add a card to the class counting strip and also fill in another number on the blank 200 chart.

Activity

Exploring Coins

Introduce students to the coins they will be using in the upcoming games. Students' experience and knowledge of coin names and coin values will vary considerably. The coin exploration and the following game, Collect 25¢, will give you opportunities to assess what students know about coins and their values.

Give 1 penny to each student. Ask students to look very closely at the coin and then turn to someone nearby and share what they noticed. As a whole class, list their observations on a piece of chart paper. Tell students that during Choice Time they will have the chance to examine other coins, such as nickels and dimes, and make a list of what's special about them.

If you find that students are engaged by examining pennies, you might want to have them examine nickels and dimes as a whole class during another session or at another time during the day.

Collect 25¢

The game Collect 25¢ can be played in pairs or small groups. Introduce the game to students.

The new activity is a game called Collect 25¢. You can play this game with a partner or with a small group of people. Each pair or group will need one number cube and a container of coins.

You may want to have a small group play a demonstration game as the rest of the class observes. Players take turns rolling the number cube and collecting the number rolled in cents. After a player rolls the number cube and takes the amount rolled, the player can trade in coins for equivalent amounts (5 pennies for 1 nickel; 1 nickel and 5 pennies for 1 dime). The first player who collects 25¢ wins.

The purpose of teaching this game in this way is to provide you with some informal assessment information about what students know about money. Expect students to vary considerably in how they play this game. Some students will collect 25¢ in pennies. Others will take a nickel when they roll a 5 and may trade pennies for other equivalent coins as they play. Try not to guide students into playing the game a particular way. If they ask you if they can trade 10 pennies for a dime, ask them if a dime is worth the same amount of money as 10 pennies.

As the small group plays in front of the class, you might involve the whole class by saying:

Jeffrey just rolled a 4 so he took 4 pennies. He already had 7 pennies. Talk with the person next to you about how much money Jeffrey has and what coins he might trade in his pennies for.

Take suggestions from a few students and then ask the player what coins can be traded for 10¢. Encourage the players involved to check each other's coins. After each player has had a turn, stop the play and ask each one how much money he or she has collected so far. You might also ask students how much more they will need to make 25¢. Continue until someone reaches 25¢.

When the game is over, discuss the names of the coins that students are using. Since all amounts rolled can be taken in pennies, it is possible to play this game successfully without knowing the names and equivalencies of all the coins. The intent of this game is to give students opportunities to share information about coin equivalencies. The more students play this game and have other opportunities to work with coins, the more likely it is that they will learn about coin equivalencies.

Variation on Collect 25¢ When students are familiar with the basic game and are comfortable with coin equivalencies, they can play Collect 50¢ with either one or two number cubes. Playing with two cubes gives students more opportunities to trade for equivalent coins.

Choice Time

Remind students about the Choice Time activities that they have worked on previously. Once again, establish expectations about how and where students will work on choices, how they will collect and put away the materials they need for each choice, and which choices students should complete by when. Students should record the choices they do each day on their Weekly Logs.

Post a list of the following choices in the classroom:

> 1. Enough for the Class?
>
> 2. Collect 25¢
>
> 3. Exploring Coins

Choice 1: Enough for the Class?

Materials: Prepared counting bags, about 10–15; Student Sheet 19, Enough for the Class? (1 per student)

Students choose a bag of objects to count. They decide whether there are enough for everyone in the class to have one and how many will be left in the bag. Depending on the number of objects, they can also determine if there would be enough for each person to have two. They write about their solution to each problem.

Choice 2: Collect 25¢

Materials: Collection of coins (1 set per 3–4 students), number cubes (1 per group of 3–4 students)

With a partner or small group, students take turns rolling a number cube and collecting that amount in coins. Coins can be traded for equivalent amounts. The object is to collect 25¢.

Choice 3: Exploring Coins

Materials: Coins (pennies, nickels, dimes), 3 sheets of chart paper labeled "Pennies," "Nickels," "Dimes"

Students examine coins and share their observations with another student. They can list their observations on chart paper.

Observing the Students

The choices in this investigation focus on counting sets of objects by 1's and by groups, and developing strategies for combining and comparing two quantities. Coins are used as a tool for modeling these important mathematical ideas. As students work at each activity, observe the following:

Enough for the Class?

- How do students count the number of objects in their bags? Do they count by 1's or by groups? Do they recognize that they would get the same amount whether they count by 1's, 2's, or 5's?

- How do students determine how many leftovers are in the bag? Do they count out a group for the class and then count the leftovers or do they count up from the total number of people in the class to the total number in the bag? (See the **Teacher Note,** Observing Students Counting, p. 91.)

Collect 25¢

■ Are students able to count out their coins accurately?

■ Do they trade coins for coins of equal value?

■ Do students collect their 25¢ in pennies, or do they know other coins that will equal 25¢?

Exploring Coins

■ What sorts of things do students notice about each coin? Do they know coin values and names?

Many Choice Time activities are designed so that students will work on them more than once. By playing a game repeatedly or by solving similar problems, students are able to refine strategies, see a variety of approaches, and bring new knowledge to familiar experiences. You may find that some students return to the same activity over and over again. Suggest to these students that they make a different first choice and then choose their favorite activity as a second choice.

Session 2 Follow-Up

 **Homework**

Exploring Coins Students investigate coins with someone at home and see if together they notice anything new. Students could also ask a grown-up for help in counting the coins in a pocket or purse. They record their work on Student Sheet 20, Exploring Coins.

 **Extension**

Number Cubes Number cubes can be made from small wooden cubes or from half-pint milk containers. Wash the container, fold down the top so that it lies flat on one side and tape it down using masking tape. The "cube" can be covered with construction or contact paper. Students can draw on dots or write numerals 1–6. Consider enlisting the help of parent volunteers to make each student a milk carton "number cube" to keep at home to use to play games such as Collect 25¢.

Observing Students Counting

Students will be counting many things during this unit and throughout the year. Counting involves more than knowing the names, the sequence, and how to write numbers. It is the basis for understanding our number system and for almost all the number work primary students do. In second grade, students will count into the hundreds, not only by 1's, but by 2's, 5's, 10's, and other numbers. Many students will use counting-on or counting-back procedures for finding answers to problems.

You can learn a lot about what students understand about counting by observing them as they work. Listen as they talk with each other. Observe them as they count orally and in writing and how they count objects. Talk with students, asking them about their thinking.

Expect a great deal of diversity. Some students may be inconsistent—successful at one time and having difficulty the next. At this point, don't worry about correcting students' mistakes or misconceptions; they will have other opportunities to count and use numbers. You may observe some of the following:

- Counting orally: Generally students can count orally farther than they can count objects or correctly write numbers. Question students to see if they can count on, for example, "Count on from 95." Most second graders can count on from any number less than 100; a few need to start over at 1 or a number such as 20.

- Counting objects: Some students may correctly count 100 or more objects; others may not consistently count 10. Some students may count the number of objects correctly when they are spread out in a line or when they physically move the object while counting, but have difficulty when the objects are in a random grouping.

- Counting by writing numbers: Many beginning second grade students can write numbers to 100 (although they may reverse numerals and/or digits). It is common for students to have difficulty counting and writing numbers greater than 100. For example, some students count to 100 and then write 200, 300, 400, and so on. Others count to 110 and then go to 200, count to 210, go to 300, and so on.

- Young students frequently reverse numbers or digits. Often this is not a mathematical problem, but a perceptual problem. Students should write numbers on the counting strips until you see how far they can reasonably go. Often students have difficulty at the "bridges" between tens, such as 19 and 20, 29 and 30, or 39 and 40.

- Counting by 2's, 5's, and other numbers: Counting by groups is different from counting by 1's. However, as in counting by 1's, students often learn the oral sequence before they are able fully to comprehend what counting by groups means. Sometimes students don't realize that the total of a quantity is the same whether it is counted by 1's, 2's, or other amounts.

Counting Strips and Counting Choices

Materials

- Prepared counting bags (10–15)
- Coin sets (1 set per 3–4 students)
- Number cubes with dots or numbers 1–6 (1 per group of 3–4 students)
- Adding-machine tape (several strips per student)
- Tape
- Student Sheet 21 (1 per student, homework)

What Happens

Students are introduced to counting strips. This activity, along with Collect 25¢, Exploring Coins, and Enough for the Class? are choices for the next two sessions. Students' work focuses on:

- counting objects
- counting orally
- writing numbers sequentially

Start-Up

Today's Number Sometime during the school day, students brainstorm ways to express the number of the days they have been in school. They add a card to the class counting line and also fill in another number on the blank 200 chart. For complete details on this routine, see p. 124.

Ask students to share what happened during the coin exploration they tried for homework. Suggest that students tell about any new characteristics of a coin they noticed, or share what they learned while counting coins or playing Collect 25¢.

Activity

Counting Strips

Today there is a new activity you can try during Choice Time. As one of your choices you can make a counting strip by writing numbers on paper strips.

Ask students how high they think they could count and write numbers.

Begin with 1 and write the numbers, one under the other, as high as you can count. Make sure you write each number large enough so that it is easy to read. If you need more paper, you can tape strips of paper together.

Demonstrate how to make a counting strip by taping a piece of adding-machine tape to the board and writing the numbers one under the other. Having students write numbers in that way helps them form more visual number patterns.

Choice Time

Students continue to work on Choice Time activities from the previous session. In addition, Counting Strips is added to the choice list.

---

1. Enough for the Class?

2. Collect 25¢

3. Exploring Coins

4. **Counting Strips**

For a review of the descriptions of Choice 1: Enough for the Class?, Choice 2: Collect 25¢, and Choice 3: Exploring Coins, see p. 89.

Choice 4: Counting Strips

Materials: Adding-machine tape cut into strips about 2 feet long

Students write numbers as high as they are able on a long strip of paper. Strips can be rolled and secured with a paper clip to make them easier to handle and store. At the end of Session 4, plan to have a short discussion about the patterns students are noticing on their counting strips.

Observing the Students

Refer to p. 89 for suggestions on what you may want to watch for as you observe students working on the first three choices. Observation suggestions for the new activity are provided here.

Counting Strips

- How far in the counting sequence are students able to write numbers?
- Are students able to make the transitions between the tens (19, 20, . . . 29, 30, . . .)?
- Can students continue the counting sequence beyond 100? Do they have reversals? If so, what do they reverse?
- Do students recognize any patterns in the counting sequence? Do they use these patterns as they write the numbers?

Temara	Ebony	Simon
83	97	1
84	98	2
85	99	3
86	100	4
87	200	5
88	300	6
89	400	7
90	500	8
91	600	9
92	700	10
93	800	11
94	900	12
95	1000	13
96	1200	14
97	1300	15
98	1400	16
99	1500	17
100	1600	18
1001	1700	19
1002	1800	02
1003	1900	21
1004	2000	22
1002	2100	23
1006	2200	24
1007	2300	25
1008	2400	28
1009	2500	29
10010		05
10011		32
		33
		35
		04
		14
		42
		43
		44
		45
		05
		51
		52

Class Discussion: Counting Strips

Gather students together at the end of Session 4 for a brief discussion about their counting strips. During Choice Time, you may have identified some common errors that students were making. Highlight these by putting the incorrect counting sequence on the board and asking students if they can figure out what part of your counting strip is incorrect. For example, students may have difficulty when numbers go across decades (from 19 to 20, 29 to 30, 99 to 100). You might put the following sequences on the board and discuss with students what's wrong, how they know, and how they could fix it.

90, 91, 92, 93, 94, 95, 96, 97, 98, 99,
100, 1001, 1002, 1003, 1004, 1005

90, 91, 92, 93, 94, 95, 96, 97, 98, 99,
100, 200, 300, 400, 500

Learning to write numerals in the 100's and above takes time. Until this point, students' experience with numbers in the 100's has mostly been with counting orally and not working directly with the numerals. As students become more familiar with how numbers are composed, they will begin to make more sense of how they are expressed in written numerals.

At the end of this session, remind students to record in their Weekly Logs.

Sessions 3 and 4 Follow-Up

Counting Strips Students continue counting strips at home. They record the last number reached in class at the top of Student Sheet 21 or on a new piece of adding-machine tape. At home, they continue counting where they left off at school. They can attach their homework strips to their school strips tomorrow.

 **Homework**

Enough for the Class? Revisited

Materials

- Prepared bag with cubes for class work
- Counters (cubes, coins, buttons)
- Student Sheet 19 (1 per student)
- Chart paper

What Happens

Students work on an Enough for the Class? problem that is used for assessment. They record their strategies for solving this problem and then discuss the problem as a class. Their work focuses on:

- comparing two amounts
- writing about solutions using words and numbers

Assessment

Enough for the Class?

Explain to students that during this session they will be working on an Enough for the Class? word problem. Hold up the plastic bag that you have filled with cubes of two different colors. Decide on what numbers are appropriate for students to work with. We have suggested you use a few cubes less than the number of students in your class. But you may want to use larger numbers and fill the bag with more cubes than the number of students.

As a class, count the number of blue [or other color] cubes and the number of red [or other color] cubes and record this information on the board.

We found out that there are 16 blue cubes and 13 red cubes in this bag. I'd like you to think about this information and figure out how many cubes there are in the bag and if there are enough cubes in the bag for everyone in the class to have one. If there are, how many leftovers would there be? If there are not enough cubes, how many more are needed for everyone to have one cube?

You can use any materials in the room to help you solve this problem. After you have solved the problem, write about your solution on the student sheet. Your writing should include words, numbers, or pictures that tell *how* you solved the problem.

Distribute Student Sheet 19, Enough for the Class? to each student. Students should have access to counters such as cubes, coins, or other objects and pencil and paper as they solve this problem. As they are working on the problem, observe how they approach this task.

- What materials do students use? How do they represent the problem?
- How do students approach the task? Confidently? Cautiously? In need of further support or direction from you?
- How do students find the total number of cubes in the bag? Do they replicate the number of cubes and count them all from one? Do they count on from one of the numbers? Do they solve the problem by adding the numbers mentally or on paper? Do they use pictures or tallies to replicate the problem?
- How do students determine if there are enough cubes in the bag for the class and how many extras are needed or leftovers there will be?

When students are finished writing, have them read their explanations to you. Point out places that are unclear or information that is missing and have them revise their work. However, do not tell them if they are correct or incorrect.

Commenting on students' work in this manner places the focus on the clarity of their thinking. This forces students to look again at their work and learn to ask themselves, "Does this make sense?" Also, it helps them see that an important part of mathematics is communicating your thoughts to others.

When students are finished, ask for a few volunteers to read their explanations. Encourage students with different strategies for solving the problem to share their ways with the class. Keep the sharing focused on how they solved the problem.

Before counting the number of cubes in the bag, tell students that you are interested in all of their strategies and explanations for solving this problem and that you will look carefully at each person's writing. Collect the papers so that you can look over their work and make some notes. This set of papers can be used as a source of information for you not only about the understanding of individual students but also about where your class is as a whole. The **Teacher Note**, Assessment: Enough for the Class? (p. 98), provides examples and suggestions for assessing students' work on this problem.

As a class, count the cubes in the bag and determine whether there would be enough for everyone in the class to have one. You might want to pass out a cube to everyone, thus showing how many more cubes are needed or how many cubes are left in the bag if you adjusted the numbers to fit the needs of students.

At the end of this session, students should record their activity on their Weekly Logs.

In Enough for the Class? students calculated the total number of objects in a bag and compared it to the number of people in the class to determine whether there will be enough for everyone, and the number of leftovers, or how many more will be needed in order for each person to have one. Students' approaches to solving this problem can give you information about how they count a group of objects, how they combine two groups, and how they compare two amounts.

For this problem, the teacher filled a bag with 16 blue cubes and 13 red cubes. There are 26 students in this class. The following examples of student work provide a range of responses that you might expect in a second grade classroom.

Tim's and Carla's Responses

Tim and Carla both used pictures to solve the problem. Each recorded the set of blue cubes and the set of red cubes. Neither student calcu-

lated the total number of cubes but instead matched a cube to each person in their class. Tim used figures and Carla used numbers. They then counted the leftover cubes and knew there were enough for the class with 3 left over. Both students have a workable strategy for solving this comparison problem. They are clear about the two groups being compared and what the extra cubes represent. A follow-up question might be "How can you find how many cubes there were in the bag to begin with?" or, depending on the student, "Could you use the information about the number of blue cubes and the number of red cubes to figure out how many cubes there were in the bag?"

Many students used a similar strategy of replicating the problem using cubes, then counting off 26 cubes for the students in the class and counting the leftovers.

Continued on next page

Trini's and Rosie's Responses

Trini and Rosie used similar strategies to determine if there were enough for the class. Like Tim and Carla, neither student actually figured out the total number of cubes in the bag but instead considered each part—the set of blue cubes and the set of red cubes.

Trini: I know that there are 16 blue cubes, and 16 is 10 less than 26. There are 13 red cubes, and 10 plus 3 is 13, so I can use 10 of the reds for the class. There are 3 leftover reds in the bag.

Rosie: I just thought there are 16 blue so 17, 18, 19, 20, 21, 22, 23, 24, 25, 26 [*she uses her fingers to keep track*]. I need 10 more cubes and there are 13 reds, so there is enough for the class.

Both children compared the amount they needed to one part of the amount they had and worked from there. The relationship between 16 (the number of blues) and 26 (the number of students in the class) may have in part supported this strategy. They seem to understand what it means to compare two amounts and worked with the parts instead of the whole amount.

Simon's Response

Simon used the total number of cubes to help him solve the problem. He added 16 and 13 and then compared the total of 29 to the number of students in the class.

Simon is breaking apart numbers into familiar parts and then recombining the parts in order to get the total. He indicated that "29 was 3 more than 26" and he "counted up" from 26 (27, 28, 29) as a way of figuring the difference between 26 and 29. A follow-up problem might be to give him two amounts of cubes that total 42 (18 blue and 24 red) and observe how he combines the two amounts and then how he compares this larger number (42) to the number of students in the class (26).

Simon

Blue 16 $10+10=20$
Red 13 $6+3=9$
             $20+9=29$

There are 29 in the bags There are 3 extra because 29 is 3 more than 26

I know because I conted up from 26.

INVESTIGATION 5

Collecting Data About Ourselves

What Happens

Sessions 1 and 2: Collecting and Representing Data About Ourselves   Students observe, classify, count, and record data about themselves. They play a game called Guess My Rule as a way of collecting information and then work in pairs to display that information using a graph or a picture.

Session 3: Collecting Pocket Data   Students collect another set of pocket data by counting the number of pockets being worn by the students in the class. Students compare data with that collected from the previous pocket activity. Then they generate as many ways as they can to represent Today's Number. This activity is used as a teacher checkpoint.

Sessions 4 and 5: Taking Inventories   Students brainstorm a list of items from their classroom that can be counted and organize them into categories. Pairs of students then select categories to inventory. Each pair records the information collected and then figures out the total number of items in their inventory. As a whole group, they have a brief discussion about how they counted and kept track of their inventory data. Students collect more inventory data for homework.

Session 6: Representing Inventory Data   As assessment, students make a representation of the inventory data they collected for homework. In pairs, they interpret each other's representations.

Mathematical Emphasis

- Sorting and classifying information
- Collecting, recording, and representing data
- Counting and comparing amounts
- Counting groups of objects in more than one way
- Talking and writing about problem-solving strategies

What to Plan Ahead of Time

Materials

- Paper: plain 8½" by 11" (Sessions 1–3)
- Chart paper (Sessions 1–3)
- Interlocking cubes (Sessions 1–3)
- Markers, crayons (Sessions 1, 6)
- Large jar (Session 3)
- Masking or colored tape or a rubber band that fits the jar (Session 3)
- Prepared Pocket Data Chart from previous Pocket Days (Session 3)
- Large sheets of paper, 12" by 18" (Session 6)

Other Preparation

- Duplicate the following student sheets and teaching resources (located at the end of this unit) in the following quantities. If you have Student Activity Booklets, copy only the extra materials marked with an asterisk.

For Sessions 1–2

Student Sheet 22, Tomorrow's Number Using Three Numbers (p. 211): 1 per student (homework)

For Session 3

Student Sheet 23, How Many Pockets? (p. 212): 1 per student (homework)

For Sessions 4–5

Student Sheet 24, Inventory (p. 213): 1 per student (class), 1 per student (homework), plus some extras*

- Read the **Teacher Note**, Playing Guess My Rule (p. 110), to get ready for the game. (Sessions 1–2)

Collecting and Representing Data About Ourselves

Materials

- Interlocking cubes
- Plain paper
- Markers, crayons
- Chart paper
- Student Sheet 22 (1 per student, homework)

What Happens

Students observe, classify, count, and record data about themselves. They play a game called Guess My Rule as a way of collecting information and then work in pairs to display that information using a graph or a picture. Their work focuses on:

- collecting information about a group of people
- sorting and classifying information
- counting and comparing sets of data
- using pictures, tallies, and graphs to organize and display data

Start-Up

Today's Number Sometime during the school day, students brainstorm ways to express the number of days they have been in school. They add a card to the class counting strip and also fill in another number on the blank 200 chart.

Activity

Playing Guess My Rule

Introduce this investigation to students by telling them that as part of their work in mathematics this year they will sometimes collect information about themselves and their families or about groups of people in the school. They will figure out ways to organize and describe the information to find out something about that group of people.

Scientists and mathematicians often think about how things are the same and how they are different. You might group things together in one way or sometimes in another way, depending on what you are looking for or talking about.

For example, some people might think that all second graders go together because they are in second grade. But other people might think that some first graders and some second graders belong together because they all like baseball, all read the same kinds of books, or all walk to school.

Remind students of some of the activities they have worked on in this unit that involve putting things into groups (Building Cube Things, Describing Geoblocks).

Focus on characteristics of students in your classroom to give other examples about how students might go together in different ways.

Today we are going to play a game called Guess My Rule using the people in our class. You are going to have to pay attention to a lot of different characteristics and figure out how certain groups of people go together. Let's try the game. I am going to think of a secret rule. Some people will fit my rule and some people won't. You're going to guess what my rule is.

For these two class demonstrations, choose straightforward, visually obvious rules such as WEARING A WATCH, WEARING STRIPES, or WEARING SHORT SLEEVES. Tell students that you are going to group them by a characteristic that they can see, such as hair color or what they are wearing, and not a characteristic that they can't see, such as LIKES CHOCOLATE ICE CREAM or HAS A DOG. For more information, see the **Teacher Note**, Playing Guess My Rule (p. 110).

Choose two students who fit your rule, and have them stand in a designated area where the class can see them.

I have a secret rule that tells something about people in this class. It's something you can see. Some people fit my rule and some people do not. Harris and Tory both fit my rule. Harris and Tory, please go stand by the chalkboard where everyone can see you.

Who thinks he or she knows someone who should stand with Harris and Tory? Don't tell me what my rule is yet! Right now I just want you to tell me who else you think goes in the group with these two boys.

Students take turns saying who they think might fit the rule. If the person does fit, ask him or her to stand with the others. If the person does not fit, send him or her to stand in another area designated for those who don't fit.

Stress the importance of all clues—both those that fit the rule and those that do not. Prolong the clue gathering until many students have had a chance to contribute guesses and most of the students in your class have joined one group or the other. See the **Dialogue Box**, Playing Guess My Rule (p. 112), for an example of how clues are gathered as the game progresses.

When enough evidence has been gathered and you sense that most students have a good idea of the rule, allow students to say what they think the rule is. Ask students to state the reasons for their guesses. Of course, it is possible that students will come up with categories that do fit the evidence but are not the rule you had in mind. If this happens, acknowledge the students' good thinking even though it did not lead to your secret rule.

Collecting and Recording Guess My Rule Data

Before students return to their seats, record the data about the number of people who did and did not fit the rule on chart paper so it can easily be saved. If some students are still in their seats, have them place themselves into the appropriate group and then have students count the number of people in each group.

WEARING SHORT SLEEVES: 11

NOT WEARING SHORT SLEEVES: 15

Continue playing more rounds of Guess My Rule. Play at least one game where the rule is wearing shoes with laces (you will need this information in the next activity). Each time, record the data in a different way in order to model a variety of ways of keeping track of data. You can use, for example, pictures, tallies, numbers, check marks. Students may have other suggestions for recording data. Encourage variety and innovation. Record the data on a large sheet of chart paper so it can easily be saved.

Wearing shorts	ʂ ʂ ʂ ʂ ʂ ʂ ʂ ʂ ʂ ʂ ʂ ʂ ʂ ʂ ʂ
Not wearing shorts	ʂ ʂ ʂ ʂ ʂ ʂ ʂ ʂ ʂ ʂ ʂ
Shoes with laces	√√√√√√√√√√√√√√√√√√√
Shoes without laces	√√√√√√
Wearing stripes	ꟷꟷꟷ ꟷꟷꟷ ꟷꟷꟷ I
Not wearing stripes	ꟷꟷꟷ ꟷꟷꟷ

Note: We have suggested some possible rules that can be used for collecting data. Some rules may not be descriptive of your classroom. For instance, in some schools all students might wear uniforms or students may not be allowed to wear sneakers to school. It is important to choose rules that are descriptive of the students in your class.

Looking at the collected data, ask students to figure out the number of students in each group. You might ask them to combine the totals for each rule or compare the numbers for each group.

How many more people are wearing shoes with laces than wearing shoes without laces?

If there are 28 students in our class and 10 people are wearing stripes, how many are not wearing stripes?

If no one notices, ask students why they think the total number for each data set is 28 (or whatever the total number of students in your class is).

Representing Guess My Rule Data

Working in pairs, students choose one of the data sets collected during Guess My Rule and find a way to represent the information. They can use interlocking cubes, pictures, numbers, or graphs.

Often when mathematicians collect information, they show it in different ways so that they can see the information in new ways and they can share it with other people. Sometimes mathematicians make pictures or graphs and sometimes they build models. They call these *representations* of the data.

With your partner, choose a set of data that we collected during Guess My Rule. Make your own representation of the data in a way that is different from how we recorded it on the board. You can use cubes, or draw a picture of the data. For example, if you pick WEARING A BELT, draw something so that someone who wasn't here could figure out how many people wore belts and how many did not.

Before students begin working, have them generate ideas about how they might make a representation of these data. Often the word *representation* may be unfamiliar to students. Using words like *picture, graph, chart,* or *model* along with *representation* may be helpful. As a way of getting students started, give an example like watches and solicit ideas about how they might organize a picture or graph and what materials they might use. The **Teacher Note**, Inventing Pictures of the Data (p. 111), provides some examples of pictures and graphs that second graders have made.

Make available paper, markers and crayons, and a variety of materials that students can use to make their representations. If some students are having difficulty getting started, you can help them think about which materials they might want to use, and then have them think about the two pieces of information they need to represent.

Observing the Students As students are working, circulate around the room and observe the following:

- How are students organizing the information?
- Are they accurately representing the information?
- What materials and methods have they chosen to represent the data?

Ask students to explain their representations to you.

- Can they interpret their representations?
- Can they extract the important information from their representations?

Asking students to explain their work allows you to learn more about how they are thinking and helps them to clarify their own thinking. As students talk about their work, they will correct themselves or clarify aspects that do not make sense. Encourage partners to ask each other questions about their work.

Sharing Representations   Have students briefly share their representations by asking groups that worked with the same set of data to bring their representations to the front of the room.

If you chose to represent the information about [WEARING STRIPES], bring your graphs or models up front so everyone can look at them.

Comment on the variety of representations and materials used. If you have time, ask each pair to say one thing about their representation. Find a place in the classroom to display the representations so students can get a closer look at a later time.

Waring watches

waring ⊙⊙⊙⊙
watch

not ⊙⊙⊙⊙⊙⊙⊙⊙⊙⊙
waring ⊙⊙⊙⊙⊙⊙⊙
a watch ⊙⊙⊙⊙⊙⊙⊙⊙⊙⊙

We think 4 have watches and
22 do not.

11 have brown hair
15 don't have brown hair

brown hair

not brown hair

Representing Data with Categories

When students organized their Guess My Rule Data, they were dealing with two groups, the group of people who fit the rule and the group of people who did not fit the rule. In some cases, the people in the latter category could not be described in any other way. For example, with the rule WEARING WATCHES, either students are or are not wearing watches, and the group without watches cannot further be described using the category of watches. In contrast, the students in the group WEARING SHOES WITHOUT LACES can further be described by other categories of types of shoes.

Introduce this idea to students in the following way:

Yesterday we collected some data about the number of people in our class who were wearing shoes with laces and the number of people who were not wearing shoes with laces. This gives us information about the

type of shoes worn by some students in our class, but there is a whole group of students for whom the only thing we know about them is that they were not wearing shoes with laces. What are some other categories we could use to further describe the types of shoes worn by the people in this group?

Solicit ideas from students and list them on the board or overhead. Help them organize their list of categories into a simple bar graph. Ask for students who fit each category to stand up. Draw a square, an X, or a stick figure on the graph for each student.

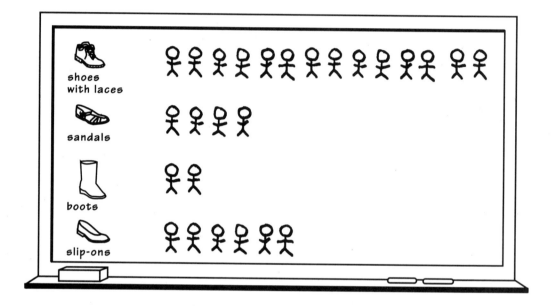

When all the data from your class have been recorded, ask students what types of things they can now tell about shoes worn by the people in their classroom.

What information does this graph tell us?

What can you say about the number of people wearing shoes with laces compared to the number of people wearing sandals?

How does this representation differ from the representation some of you made yesterday using the Guess My Rule data?

Would the data change if we collected the same information tomorrow? Why or why not?

Ask students how they might use the interlocking cubes to build a model that would represent the shoe data. Have a pair of students represent the data using the cubes.

Students will continue to collect, record, and interpret data in the next two sessions of this unit and in other units in the *Investigations* curriculum. Consider integrating data collection and representation into other areas of your curriculum, such as science or social studies. Collecting data about themselves is a wonderful way to help students get to know one another at the beginning of the school year.

Sessions 1 and 2 Follow-Up

Tomorrow's Number Using Three Numbers   After Session 1, students record tomorrow's number on Student Sheet 22, Tomorrow's Number Using Three Numbers. For homework, they think of ways to make Tomorrow's Number using three numbers and addition and/or subtraction.

 **Homework**

Guess My Rule is a classification game in which players try to figure out the common characteristic, or attribute, of a set of objects. To play the game, the rule maker (who may be you, a student, or a small group) decides on a secret rule for classifying a particular group of things. For example, rules for people might be WEARING BLUE or HAS GLASSES.

The rule maker starts the game by giving some examples of people who fit the rule—for example, by having two students who are wearing blue stand up. The guessers then try to find other individuals who might fit the rule: "Does Ebony fit your rule?"

With each guess, the individual named is added to one group or the other—*does fit* or *does not fit the rule*. Both groups must be clearly visible to the guessers so they can make use of all the evidence—what does and does not fit—as they try to figure out what the rule is.

You'll need to stress two guidelines during play:

■ *"Wrong" guesses are clues and just as important as "right" guesses.* "No, Bjorn doesn't fit, but that's important evidence. Think about how Graham is different from Karina, Juanita, Ping, and Jeffrey." This is a wonderful way to help students learn that errors can be important sources of information.

■ *When you think you know what the rule is, test your theory by giving another example, not by revealing the rule.* "Carla, you look like you're sure you know what the rule is. We don't want to give it away yet, so let's test your theory. Tell me someone who you think fits the rule." Requiring students to add new evidence, rather than making a guess, serves two purposes. It allows students to test their theories without revealing their guess to other students, and it provides more information and more time to think for students who do not yet have a theory.

When students begin choosing rules they sometimes think of rules that are either too vague (WEARING DIFFERENT COLORS) or too hard to guess (HAS A BUTTON MISSING FROM HIS SHIRT). Guide and support students in choosing rules that are "medium hard"—not so obvious that everyone will see them immediately but not so hard that no one will be able to figure them out.

Students should be clear about who would fit their rule *and* who would not fit; this eliminates rules like WEARING DIFFERENT COLORS, which everyone probably fits. It's also important to pick a rule about something people can observe. One rule for classifying might be PLAYS SOCCER, but no one will be able to guess this rule by just looking.

Guess My Rule can be dramatic. Keep the mystery and drama high with remarks such as, "That was an important clue," "I think Imani has a good idea now," and "I bet I know what Angel's theory is."

It is surprising how hard it can be to guess what seems to be an obvious rule like (HAS LONG HAIR). It is often difficult to predict which rules will be hard to guess. A rule you think will be tough could be guessed right away; while a rule that seemed obvious will be impossible to guess.

Give additional clues when students are truly stuck. For example, one teacher chose WEARING SHIRT WITH WORDS as the rule. All students had been placed in one of the two groups, but still no one could guess. So the teacher moved among the students, drawing attention to each in turn: "Look carefully at Jess's front. Now I'm going to turn Helena around to the back, like this—see what you can see. Look along Lila's shoulder." Finally, students guessed the rule.

Classification is a process used in many disciplines, and you can easily adapt Guess My Rule to other subject areas. Animals, states, historical figures, geometric shapes, and types of food can all be classified in different ways.

Inventing Pictures of the Data

When students invent their own individual ways of representing their data, they often come up with wonderful pictures or graphs that powerfully communicate the meaning of the data. While many commonly used representations, such as bar graphs and tallies, gradually become familiar to students, encourage them to use their own inventiveness and creativity to develop pictures and graphs as well. In this way, students make the data their own.

In the ongoing history of visual representation of data, many unusual forms of graphs and diagrams have been developed. Some of the most striking graphs were devised by a statistician or scientist to represent a single, unusual data set in a new way. Even now, new standard forms are taking their place in the statistician's repertoire beside the more familiar bar graph or histogram.

So while we do want students to use and interpret standard forms of graphs, we also want them to learn that, like other mathematicians and scientists, they can picture data in their own individual ways. These pictures or diagrams or graphs are tools in the data analysis process. Through constructing their own representations, students can become more familiar with the data, understand the data better, begin to develop theories about the data, and, if they are going to "publish" their findings, communicate what they know about the data to an audience.

Graphs can be made with pencil and paper, interlocking cubes, and stick-on notes. Cubes and stick-on notes offer flexibility since they can easily be rearranged. Encourage students to construct concrete and pictorial representations of their data using interlocking cubes, pictures, or even the actual objects.

Encourage students to invent and use different forms until they discover some that work well in organizing their data. Students in the second grade are capable of inventing simple—but effective—sketches and pictures of the data they collect. Shown on this page are some of the ways second graders have represented their Guess My Rule data. None of these exactly follows a standard graph or table form, but both show the data clearly and effectively.

DIALOGUE BOX

Playing Guess My Rule

This class is playing Guess My Rule (p. 102) and the teacher's secret rule is WEARING STRIPES.

I'm thinking of a secret rule. It is something that can be seen on some people in the class. Karina and Franco and Jeffrey, you all fit my secret rule. Please stand by the window. I want to give you one more clue. Tory and Jess do not fit my rule. Would you both go and stand by the door? Who thinks they know someone else who might belong to one of these groups? Don't guess the rule; just tell me another person you think might fit.

Olga: Oh I know it, I know it. The rule is . . .

Careful not to say the rule just yet. Instead, can you name someone in the class who fits the rule?

Olga: Simon fits the rule. He definitely fits the rule.

OK, Simon go and stand with the group by the window. You fit my rule. [*Simon joins Karina, Franco, and Jeffrey. In addition to wearing stripes (the secret rule), all four students are wearing blue jeans.*]

Ping: [*who is also wearing blue jeans but not stripes*] Oh now I know the rule. I think I fit the rule. Do I?

No, Ping does not fit the rule I am thinking of. Ping, you should join the group standing by the door. Ping is an important piece of information.

[*Laura is sitting at a table with five other students. None of these students are wearing stripes.*]

Laura: I don't think anyone at my table fits the rule. [*The group nods in agreement, and they join the group standing by the door.*]

So now we have about half of our class in one group or the other. I can tell by your hands that many of you think you know what my secret rule is. As I call your name, please place yourself in one of the groups. If you think you fit my rule, stand by the window, and if you think you do not fit my rule, stand near the door.

[*A few students at a time place themselves in one of the two groups. With the addition of new students who are wearing stripes, the characteristic of wearing blue jeans is less obvious.*]

OK, now that everyone is in a group, I'd like you to turn to the person next to you and tell them what you think my secret rule is.

In this conversation, the teacher keeps the focus on looking carefully at all the evidence, rather than on getting the right answer quickly. She uses Ping's sensible guess to point out the value of negative information: Even though Ping does not fit the rule, he provides an important clue in narrowing down the possibilities. By prolonging the discussion and gathering more clues, the teacher gives more students time to think and reach their own conclusions. Her choice to have all students place themselves in one of the two groups allows for the inclusion of every student in this activity. Rather than calling on just one student to reveal the mystery clue of WEARING STRIPES, she decides to have students share their ideas with a partner, thus allowing many students to participate in the excitement of revealing the clue.

Session 3

Collecting Pocket Data

Materials

- Interlocking cubes
- Jar marked with previous level of cubes
- Masking or colored tape or rubber band
- Pocket Data Chart from previous pocket activity
- Chart paper
- Student Sheet 23 (1 per student, homework)
- Plain paper

What Happens

Students collect another set of pocket data by counting the number of pockets being worn by the students in the class. Students compare data with that collected from the previous pocket activity. Then they generate as many ways as they can to represent Today's Number. This activity is used as a teacher checkpoint. Students' work focuses on:

- collecting data
- counting and comparing data
- combining and comparing numbers
- expressing a number in more than one way

To help students get to know and become comfortable with the pocket routine, the basic structure of this session is similar to their initial experience with How Many Pockets? in Investigation 2 of this unit. Now, however, students begin to compare data when they note how the number of pockets has changed from the previous Pocket Day. Post or rewrite the Pocket Data Chart showing the pocket counts from previous days and display the empty jar with the cube level marked. Revisit the data and then pose a new problem.

The last time we counted pockets, our class was wearing (for example) **42 pockets. Do you think we will be wearing more, fewer, or about the same number of pockets today? Why?**

Ask students to explain their reasoning, which may include attendance, a change in the weather, or their anticipation of Pocket Day. Then ask students to estimate the number of pockets.

How many pockets do you think we are wearing today?

Record students' estimates on the chalkboard or chart paper. Then pass around containers of cubes and have each student take the same number of cubes as he or she has pockets. Before collecting the cubes, point out to students the level of cubes that filled the jar on the previous Pocket Day.

The last time we counted pockets, the cubes filled the jar to here. I wonder if the level will be higher, lower, or about the same today? Let's see.

As you call out numbers of pockets, those students who have that many pockets should put their cubes in the jar. When all the cubes have been collected, hold up the jar so that all can see it.

Activity

How Many Pockets?

How full is the jar now? How does this compare with the last time, when we had 42 pockets? Do we have more, fewer, or about the same number of pockets today?

Invite students to change their estimates if they wish to do so. Some may wish to revise their thinking, based on what they now know about the number of cubes in the jar. Other students will need more experiences working with quantities to develop these number relationships. Mark the new level with tape or a rubber band.

How can we use the cubes to find out exactly how many pockets we are wearing today?

Explain that you want to count in two different ways to be sure their count is accurate. Decide on the two ways you will count the cubes (e.g., by 1's, 2's, or 5's), then together count the cubes in each way.

Comparing the Data Add the day's total number of pockets to the Pocket Data chart. (Also note the number of students present.)

We wrote 42 on the chart on our first Pocket Day and 54 today. What do those numbers tell us? Are we wearing more or fewer pockets today than we wore on the last Pocket Day?

To facilitate discussion, you might build a train of connecting cubes for each number. Have the whole group count aloud to the first pocket total, then the second total, as you and a volunteer connect cubes for each train. As students compare the completed trains, they are likely to comment that "one train is longer" or "one train has more cubes."

How might we use these trains to figure out how many more [or fewer] pockets we have today than before?

Direct comparison is often a helpful way for students to compare two quantities. Some students will see the difference as how much longer one train is than the other and count the extra cubes on the longer train. Other students might compare by looking at how many more cubes it would take to make the shorter train the same length as the longer train. If you wish, you also might record the pocket data on an index card and tack it up under Today's Number on the class counting strip. Record the number of people present for this pocket activity.

Call students' attention to the number of days in school. If you have not posted Today's Number and filled in the number chart, do so now. As you fill in the number on the chart, ask questions such as:

How many more days until we will be in school 30 days? How can you tell?
How many more days until we will be in school 40 days?
Which block will I fill in when we are in school 35 days? How can you tell?

Give paper to each student and ask them to generate all the number sentences they can think of to represent Today's Number. Each student should make his or her own record of these number sentences.

Ten minutes before the end of the session, call students together. Label chart paper with the numeral and the number word, and list the students' ways to express the number. As number sentences are shared, some students may realize that they have made a mistake. Ask them to correct their mistake above their original sentence. Explain that this will help you when you look back over their work at a later time.

Ask students if they notice any patterns in any of the combinations. They may say, for example, that when you are adding two numbers, if one of the addends increases by 1 and the other decreases by 1, then the answer remains the same.

$$13 + 7 = 20$$
$$14 + 6 = 20$$

Talk about combinations that reflect a breaking down of a larger number.

$$10 + 10 = 20$$
$$6 + 4 + 6 + 4 = 20$$

Some students may also recognize subtraction patterns that involve increasing both numbers by the same amount.

$$23 - 3 = 20$$
$$33 - 13 = 20$$

Ask students to put these papers in their math folders. At the end of this unit, you may want to look back at two or three examples of student records of Today's Number as a way of assessing their progress.

At the end of the session, remind students to fill in their Weekly Logs.

Session 3 Follow-Up

How Many Pockets?   Students are given a total number of pockets (20) that five children are wearing. They figure out three possible ways the 20 pockets could be distributed among the five children. They record their work on Student Sheet 23, How Many Pockets?

 **Homework**

Taking Inventories

Materials

- Student Sheet 24 (1 per student, class; 1 per student, homework; and some extras)

What Happens

Students brainstorm a list of items from their classroom that can be counted and organize them into categories. Pairs of students then select categories to inventory. Each pair records the information collected and then figures out the total number of items in their inventory. As a whole group, they have a brief discussion about how they counted and kept track of their inventory data. Students collect more inventory data for homework. Their work focuses on:

- counting a set of objects
- choosing categories to classify a set of objects
- recording and keeping track of a data set

Start-Up

Today's Number Sometime during the school day, students brainstorm ways to express the number of days they have been in school. Suggest that students use both addition and subtraction in each expression. Add a card to the class counting strip, and fill in another number on the blank 200 chart.

What Can We Count?

During the next two sessions, students work in pairs to count items in their classroom. Introduce the activity by asking students about the word *inventory*.

Has anyone ever heard the word *inventory*?

If students are unfamiliar with this word, offer a context such as:

Often stores close for a day each year and take an inventory of what is in the store. A toy store might have lots of stuffed animals, but the owners need to know what *kinds* of stuffed animals they have. So the employees make a list of all the kinds of stuffed animals. In addition to knowing what kinds of toys they have, store owners may also want to know *how many* of each kind of animal they have. So the employees count each kind of animal. During inventories, a lot of counting is done. By taking an inventory, the store owners can keep track of what is in the store and what new things they might want to buy or replace.

Explain to students that inventories are also used to help people keep track of information. Connect their previous experiences with Guess My Rule and collecting data about people as a type of inventory.

Suppose we were going to take an inventory of our classroom. What are some things in our classroom that we could count?

As students brainstorm, list their ideas on the board. Encourage them to focus on objects that are in the classroom, as opposed to items that are on people (watches, glasses). Ask students which of the items they think would be easy to count, and which might be more difficult to count and why.

As a way of organizing the task of taking an inventory, introduce students to the idea of putting things into categories. Use a statement such as the following, modifying it to fit the list your students have generated.

I'm noticing that some of the things you have mentioned to count could go together. For example, benches, stools, and chairs are all things that we can sit on. What are some other groups of things on this list that seem to go together?

As a way of defining categories, have students make suggestions about things that go together. The **Dialogue Box**, Choosing Things to Inventory (p. 121), illustrates how one teacher helped the class break apart a large category into two smaller ones.

List on the board the categories and the items that students suggest. For example:

FURNITURE	THINGS YOU WRITE WITH	THINGS YOU SIT ON
desks	pencils	chairs
tables	markers	benches
bookshelves	chalk	stools
chairs		

Decide on five or six categories of things to inventory. In this way, several students can work on counting the same group of objects. Later in the session, they can use this information as they share strategies for counting and keeping track.

Some of the items students suggest will be challenging to count for different reasons. Items such as books, connecting cubes, crayons (if they are stored in a large container), and pattern blocks are challenging because there are large quantities of them. Try to keep the number of items that students count under 100. You might suggest to students (or ask students to suggest) ways of making these items more manageable to count.

Often these items can be further categorized. For example, books could be categorized by topic, or by hard or soft cover, pattern blocks by shape, and cubes by color. Students need not count the entire set of these objects but might count a subset, such as a bucket or box of cubes or a bookshelf of books. Items such as chairs or furniture might be challenging, not because of the quantity, but because it is difficult to keep track of what has and has not been counted. Ask students to share ideas about how they might count and keep track of these items as they take their inventory.

Activity

Taking a Classroom Inventory

Distribute Student Sheet 24, Inventory, to each student. Working in pairs, students choose a category listed on the board that they would like to inventory. Students should write the category at the top of their student sheet, then list the groups within that category. As they inventory the items within each group, they should record the amount. When they are finished counting each group, they should figure out the total number of items in their inventory.

Observing the Students As students work on their inventories, observe the following:

- How do students organize the task?
- How do they count the objects?
- What strategies do students have or develop for keeping track of their count?
- How do they record the information they collect?
- How do they figure out the total amount of items?

Since students work together in pairs quite often throughout the *Investigations* curriculum, you may be interested in watching how partners interact, how they make decisions, and how or if they work as a team. Working together cooperatively on a shared project is something that students learn to do over time and by having many opportunities to do so.

If pairs of students finish early, suggest that they choose another category of items to inventory.

Class Discussion: How Did You Count?

Counting and keeping track of the count is an important aspect of collecting data. One aspect of counting accurately is developing strategies for keeping track of what has been counted and what still needs to be counted. As counting situations arise in your classroom, encourage students to share strategies for counting and tracking their count.

Near the end of the session, discuss with students how they counted their inventories.

When you were taking your inventory and had to count a large number of items, did you use any special strategy for counting and keeping track of what you counted?

Some students will probably offer ideas such as putting items into groups or moving objects from one place to another. Other students might describe a systematic way of keeping track. One second grader counted the chairs in the room by, "starting on one side of the room and making check marks on my clipboard and when I got to the door I knew I was finished."

If different pairs of students counted the same item, have them share their results. Discuss why there may be discrepancies between their counts.

When Carla and Temara counted the books in the bookcase, they counted 87. Tim and Paul counted 75 books in the same bookcase. Why do you think they may have different counts?

Students discuss various reasons for the discrepancy, such as that they may have counted the books at different times so that the number of books changed, and it is easy to lose track when counting and to make mistakes. The focus of the discussion should be on ways of organizing the counting process and keeping track, rather than on who counted correctly. Encourage students to think about ways of making sure their counts are accurate, such as grouping into 5's or 10's and checking their counts. Students in one second grade class found that their counts were more accurate when they counted items by 2's and 5's rather than by 1's.

At the end of the session, remind students to record their work in their Weekly Logs.

Sessions 4 and 5 Follow-Up

Homework

Inventory   At the end of Session 4, students inventory something at home. Explain that they will need this information for the day after tomorrow (Session 6). Each student will need a copy of Student Sheet 24, Inventory, to record the data. Spend a few minutes brainstorming categories of things that students might inventory at home. Some ideas might include: types of silverware, types of videotapes, pictures, number of light switches on each floor, stuffed animals, types of shirts, and collections (coins, baseball cards, shells).

Extension

People Inventory   Begin an inventory of special characteristics that describe the people in the classroom. For example:

There are 29 people in the classroom.

There are 13 boys and 16 girls.

We have 18 sisters and 26 brothers.

15 people in our class have pets. We have 8 dogs, 7 cats, 9 gerbils, 1 snake, and 40 fish.

Each day you might collect different data from the class and list the information on chart paper. Depending on the information, data can be collected in various ways: by raising hands, making cube trains, or making tallies to indicate amounts. Students can make suggestions of things to inventory. The class could make a book using this information.

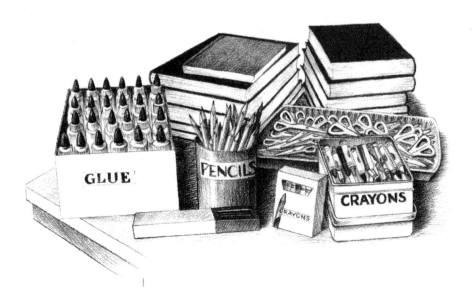

Choosing Things to Inventory

Grouping items into categories can be a challenging task. In this discussion, the teacher helps students narrow their list of inventory items by breaking a large category into smaller groups. Students are encouraged to look for similarities among items as they prepare their list of things to inventory in the classroom (p. 116). Students have brainstormed an extensive list of items.

Naomi suggested that one thing we could inventory in our classroom is things on the wall. Take a look at the list. What items could be included in that group?

Bjorn: Maps, pictures, the schedules, the calendar.

Lila: Posters, the attendance chart, alphabet cards, and some of our writing papers.

That's a lot of things. Let's think about pictures. What sorts of pictures are on our walls?

Paul: There are pictures we painted.

Carla: And there are the pattern block designs, those are sort of like pictures. And photographs of other countries.

So, even in the group PICTURES there are many different kinds. And all of these belong to a bigger group, THINGS THAT HANG ON THE WALL. [*Teacher writes PICTURES on the board and underneath lists the groups students have mentioned.*]

You also mentioned things like maps, calendars, and schedules. What are those used for?

Graham: They tell you things like where places are and when things are happening.

Angel: They give you information about different stuff.

What if we had a category called GIVES YOU INFORMATION? What things would go in this group?

Ayaz: Maps and the schedules.

Ebony: I think the Today's Number charts, where we do the number of the day, gives you information. And there are a lot of those!

Tim: The alphabet cards and also those handwriting cards, because that gives you information about how to write letters.

Linda: Some of these things will be easy to count because there are only one or two of them, but others will be harder.

[*The teacher makes a list on the board. Next to PICTURES she writes:*]

GIVES YOU INFORMATION
maps
schedules
Today's Number
alphabet cards
handwriting cards

So, now we have two groups of things that we could inventory in our classroom and both of them belong to a bigger group—the group THINGS THAT HANG ON THE WALL.

PICTURES
paintings
chalk
pattern block designs
photos

Representing Inventory Data

Materials

- Large sheets of paper, 12" by 18" or larger (1 per student)
- Crayons or markers

What Happens

As assessment, students make a representation of the inventory data they collected for homework. In pairs, they interpret each other's representations. Their work focuses on:

- representing a set of data
- comparing data representations

Activity

Assessment

Representing Home Inventories

For this session, students will need the data they collected from the inventory they did at home for homework. If some students do not have this information, they can make a representation of the inventory data they collected in school during Sessions 4 and 5.

Last night, you took an inventory of something in your house. Today, you are going to make a picture or a representation of that information.

Remind students about representations they made during this investigation for the Guess My Rule data.

Your picture or representation should show all the different groups of things you counted and how many there were of each item. Just by looking at your picture, someone should be able to tell what information you collected.

Using examples of representations of Guess My Rule, point out to students important aspects of representation, such as identifying what the different groups are and being able to count how many things (or people) were in each group. Choose different types of representations as examples so that students realize that there is more than one way to make a representation.

For most of this session, students work on representing their inventory data. Circulate around the room as they work, encouraging them to explain their representations to you. There will be a wide variety of approaches to this task. Some students will have systematic ways of keeping track of their data, while others will not manage to show every piece of data. Some students will use pictures to stand for each piece of data, while others might choose to use tallies or boxes.

Representing data develops over time. Students benefit not only from their own experiences in organizing and representing data but also from experiences and representations shared by others. If you are doing the full-year *Investigations* curriculum, students will be involved with collecting and representing data in the units *Does It Walk, Crawl, or Swim?* and *How Many Pockets? How Many Teeth?* Inventory representations should be saved as part of a student's portfolio so that you can compare this early representation to the student's later work with collecting and representing data.

As students finish, suggest that they pair up and look at each other's graphs. Encourage them to try to understand their partner's representation by asking themselves the following questions:

- What is this representation about?
- What types of groups were inventoried?
- How many of each item are there?

Leave about 10 minutes at the end of this session for students to share their representations of their home inventories with the class.

Choosing Student Work to Save

As the unit ends, you may want to use one of the following options for creating a record of students' work on this unit.

- Students look back through their folders or notebooks and think about what they learned in this unit, what they remember most, and what was hard or easy for them. You might have students discuss this with partners or have students share in the whole group.

- Depending on how you organize and collect student work, you may want to have students select some examples of their work to keep in a math portfolio. In addition, you may want to choose some examples from each student's folder to include. Items such as Today's Number and the Enough for the Class? assessments, their inventory representation, and Student Sheets 11 and 12, Ways to Fill, can be useful pieces for assessing student growth over the school year.

- Send a selection of work home for parents to see. Students write a cover letter, describing their work in this unit. This work should be returned if you are keeping a year-long portfolio of mathematics work for each student.

Today's Number

Today's Number is one of the routines that are built into the grade 2 *Investigations* curriculum. Routines provide students with regular practice in important mathematical ideas such as number combinations, counting and estimating data, and concepts of time. For Today's Number, which is done daily (or most days), students write equations that equal the number of days they have been in school. Each day, the class generates ways to make that number. For example, on the tenth day of school, students look for ways to combine numbers and operations to make 10.

This routine gives students an opportunity to explore some important ideas in number. By generating ways to make the number of the day, they explore:

- number composition and part-whole relationships (for example, 10 can be $4 + 6$, $5 + 5$, or $20 - 10$)

- equivalent arithmetical expressions

- different operations

- ways of deriving new numerical expressions by systematically modifying prior ones (for example, $5 + 5 = 10$, so $11 = 5 + 6$)

Students' strategies evolve over time, becoming more sophisticated as the year progresses. Early in the year, second graders use familiar numbers and combinations, such as $5 + 5 = 10$. As they become accustomed to the routine, they begin to see patterns in the combinations and have favorite kinds of number sentences. Later in the year, they draw on their experiences and increased understanding of number. For example on the forty-ninth day, they might include $100 - 51$, or even $1000 - 951$ in their list of ways to make 49. The types of number sentences that students contribute over time can provide you with a window into their thinking and levels of understanding of number.

If you are doing the full-year grade 2 curriculum, Today's Number is introduced in the first unit, *Mathematical Thinking at Grade 2*. Throughout the curriculum, variations are often introduced as whole-class activities and then carried on in the Start-Up section. The Start-Up section at the beginning of most sessions offers suggestions for how variations and extensions of Today's Number might be used.

While it is important to do Today's Number every day, it is not necessary to do it during math time. In fact, many teachers have successfully included Today's Number as part of their regular routines at the beginning or end of each day. Other teachers incorporate Today's Number into the odd 10 or 15 minutes that exist before lunch or before a transition time.

The basic activity is described below, followed by suggested variations. If you are not doing the full grade 2 curriculum, we suggest that you begin with the basic activity and then add variations when students become familiar with this routine.

Materials

- Chart paper
- Interlocking cubes
- Strips of adding-machine tape
- Index cards (cut in half and numbered with the days of school so far, for example, 1 through 5 for the first week of school)
- Student Sheet 1, Weekly Log
- 100 Chart (two taped together to form a 10-by-20 chart)

Basic Activity

Initially, you will want to use Today's Number in a whole group, starting the first week of school. After a short time, students will be familiar with the routine and be ready to use it independently.

Establishing the Routine

Step 1. Post the chart paper. Call the students' attention to the small box on their Weekly Log in which they have been recording the number of days they have been in school.

Continued on next page

Step 2. Record Today's Number. Write the number of the day at the top of the chart paper. Ask students to suggest ways of making that total.

Step 3. List the number sentences students suggest. Record their suggestions on chart paper. As you do so, invite the group to confirm each suggestion or discuss any incorrect responses and to explain their thinking. You might have cubes available for students to double-check number sentences.

Step 4. Introduce the class counting strip. Show students the number cards you made and explain that the class is going to create a counting strip. Each day, the number of the day will be added to the row of cards. Post the cards in order in a visible area.

Step 5. Introduce the 200 chart. Display the blank chart and explain that another way the class will keep track of the days in school will be by filling in the chart. Record the appropriate numbers in the chart. Tell the class that the number of each day will be added to the chart. To help bring attention to landmark numbers on the chart, ask questions such as, "How many more days until the tenth day of school? the twentieth day?"

Variations

If you choose not to use the number of days students have been in school, but still want to use this activity, try using the calendar date. For example, on September 14, use 14 as Today's Number.

When students are familiar with the structure of this routine, you can connect it to the number work they are doing in particular units.

Make Today's Number Ask students to use some of the following to represent the number:

- only addition
- only subtraction
- both addition and subtraction
- three numbers

- combinations of 10 ($23 = 4 + 6 + 4 + 6 + 3$ or $23 = 1 + 9 + 2 + 8 + 3$)
- a double ($36 = 18 + 18$ or $36 = 4 + 4 + 5 + 5 + 9 + 9$)
- multiples of 5 and 10 ($52 = 10 + 10 + 10 + 10 + 10 + 2$ or $52 = 5 + 15 + 20 + 10 + 2$)
- the idea of working backward. Put the number sentences for Today's Number on the board and ask students to determine what day you are expressing: $10 + 3 + 5 + 7 + 5 + 4 = ?$ Notice how students add up this string of numbers. Do they use combinations of 10 or doubles to help them?

In addition to defining how Today's Number is expressed, you can vary how and when the activity is done:

Start the Day with Today's Number Post the day's chart paper ahead of time. When students begin arriving, they can generate number sentences and check them with partners, then record their ways to make the number of the day before school begins. Students can review the list of ways to make the number at that time or at the beginning of math class. At whole-group or morning meetings, add the day's number to the 200 chart and the counting strip.

Choice Time Post chart paper with the Number of the Day written on it so that it is accessible to students. As one of their choices, students generate number sentences and check them with partners, then record them on the chart paper.

Work with a Partner Each student works with a partner for 5 to 10 minutes and lists some ways to make the day's number. Partners check each other's work. Pairs bring their lists to the class meeting or sharing time. Students put their lists of number sentences in their math folders. These can be used as a record of students' growth in working with numbers over the school year.

Continued on next page

Homework   Assign Today's Number as homework. Students share number sentences sometime during class the following day.

Catch Up   It can be easy to get a few days behind in this routine, so here are two ways to catch up. Post two or three Number-of-the-Day pages for students to visit during Choice Time or free time. Or assign a Number of the Day to individual students. Each can generate number sentences for his or her number as well as collect number sentences from classmates.

Class History   Post "special messages" below the day's number card to create a timeline about your class. Special messages can include birthdays, teeth lost, field trips, memorable events, as well as math riddles.

Today's Number Book   Collect the Today's Number charts in a *Number-of-the-Day Book.* Arrange the pages in order, creating chapters based on 10's. Chapter 1, for example, is ways to make the numbers 1 through 10, and combinations for numbers 11–20 become Chapter 2.

How Many Pockets?

How Many Pockets? is one of the classroom routines presented in the grade 2 *Investigations* curriculum. In this routine, students collect, represent, and interpret numerical data about the number of pockets everyone in the class is wearing on a particular day. This often becomes known as Pocket Day. In addition to providing opportunities for comparison of data, Pocket Day provides a meaningful context in which students work purposefully with counting and grouping. Pocket Day experiences contribute to the development of students' number sense—the ability to use numbers flexibly and to see relationships among numbers.

If you are doing the full-year grade 2 curriculum, collect pocket data at regular intervals throughout the year. Many teachers collect pocket data every tenth day of school.

The basic activity is described below, followed by suggested variations. Variations are introduced within the context of the *Investigations* units. If you are not doing the full-year curriculum, begin with the basic activity and add variations when students become familiar with this routine.

Materials

- Interlocking cubes
- Large jar
- Large rubber band or tape
- Hundred Number Wall Chart and Number Cards (1–100)
- Pocket Data Chart (teacher-made)
- Class list of names
- Chart paper

1	2	3	4	5	6	7	8	9	10
11	12	13	14	15	16	17	18	19	20
21	22	23	24	25	26	27	28	29	30
31	32	33	34	35	36	37	38	39	40
41	42	43	44	45	46	47	48	49	50
51	52	53	54	55	56	57	58	59	60
61	62	63	64	65	66	67	68	69	70
71	72	73	74	75	76	77	78	79	80
81	82	83	84	85	86	87	88	89	90
91	92	93	94	95	96	97	98	99	100

Hundred Number Wall Chart

How many pockets are we wearing today?

	Pockets	People
Pocket Day 1		

Pocket Data Chart

Basic Activity

Step 1. Students estimate how many pockets the class is wearing today. Students share their estimates and their reasoning. Record the estimates on chart paper. As the Pocket Days continue through the year, students may base their estimates on the data recorded on past Pocket Days.

Continued on next page

Step 2. Students count their pockets. Each student takes one interlocking cube for each pocket he or she is wearing.

Step 3. Students put the cubes representing their pockets in a large jar. Vary the way in which you do this. For example, rather than passing the jar around the group, call on students with specific numbers of pockets to put their cubes in the jar (for example, students with 3 pockets). Use numeric criteria to determine who puts their cubes in the jar (for example, students with more than 5 but fewer than 8 pockets).

Step 4. With students, agree on a way to count the cubes. Count the cubes to find the total number of pockets. Ask students for ideas about how to double-check the count. By re-counting in another way, students see that a group of objects can be counted in more than one way; for example, by 1's, 2's, 5's, and 10's. With many experiences, they begin to realize that some ways of counting are more efficient than others and that a group of items can be counted in ways other than by 1, without changing the total.

Primary students are usually most secure in counting by 1's, and that is often their method of choice. Experiences with counting and grouping in other ways help them begin to see that number is conserved or remains the same regardless of its arrangement—15 cubes is 15 whether counted by 1's, 2's, or 5's. Students also become more flexible in their ability to use grouping, which is especially important in our number system, in which grouping by 10 is key.

Step 5. Record the total for the day on a Pocket Data Chart. Maintaining a chart of the pocket data as they are accumulated provides natural opportunities for students to see that data can change over time and to compare quantities.

How many pockets are we wearing today?		
	Pockets	People
Pocket Day 1	41	29

Variations

Comparing Data Students revisit the data from the previous Pocket Day and the corresponding cube level marked on the now-empty jar.

On the last Pocket Day, we counted [give number] pockets. Do you think we will be wearing more, fewer, or about the same number of pockets today? Why?

After students explain their reasoning, continue with the basic activity. When the cubes have been collected, invite students to compare the level of cubes now with the previous level and to revise their estimates based on this visual information.

Discuss the revised estimates and then complete the activity. After you add the day's total to the Pocket Data Chart, ask students to compare and interpret the data. To facilitate discussion, build a train of interlocking cubes for today's and the previous Pocket Day's number. As students compare the trains, elicit what the cube trains represent and why they have different numbers of cubes.

Continued on next page

Using the Hundred Number Wall Chart Do the basic activity, but this time students choose only one way to count the cubes. Then introduce the Hundred Number Wall Chart as a tool that can be used for counting cubes. This is easiest when done with students sitting on the floor in a circle.

To check our pocket count, we'll put our cubes in the pockets on the chart. A pocket can have just one cube, so we'll put one cube in number 1's pocket, the next cube in number 2's pocket, and keep going in the same way. How many cubes can we put in the first row?

Students will probably see that 10 cubes will fill the first row of the chart.

One group of 10 cubes fits in this row. What if we complete the second row? How many rows of the chart do you think we will fill with the cubes we counted today?

Encourage students to share their thinking. Then have them count with you and help to place the cubes one by one in the pockets on the chart. When finished, examine the chart together, pointing out the total number of cubes in it and the number of complete rows. For each row, snap together the cubes to make a train of 10. As you do so, use the rows to encourage students to consider combining groups of 10. Record the day's total on the Pocket Data Chart.

Note: If cubes do not fit in the pockets of the chart, place the chart on the floor and place the cubes on top of the numbers.

Finding the Most Common Number of Pockets
Each student connects the cubes representing his or her pockets into a train. Before finding the total number of pockets, sort the cube trains with students to find out what is the most common number of pockets. Pose and investigate additional questions, such as:

■ **How many people are wearing the greatest number of pockets?**

■ **Is there a number of pockets no one is wearing?**

■ **Who has the fewest pockets?**

The cubes are then counted to determine the total number of pockets.

Taking a Closer Look at Pocket Data Each student builds a cube train representing his or her pockets. Beginning with those who have zero pockets, call on students to bring their cube trains to the front of the room. Record the information in a chart such as the one shown here. You might make a permanent chart with blanks for placing number cards.

_O_ people have 0 pockets.	_O pockets_
_4_ people have 1 pocket.	_4_ pockets
_2_ people have 2 pockets.	_4_ pockets
_2_ people have 3 pockets.	_6 pockets_

Pose questions about the data, such as, "Two people each have 2 pockets. How many pockets is that?" Then record the number of pockets.

To work with combining groups, you might keep a running total of pockets as data are recorded in the chart until you have found the cumulative total.

We counted 12 (for example) pockets, and then we counted 6 pockets. How many pockets have we counted so far? Be ready to tell us how you thought about it.

As students give their solutions, encourage them to share their mental strategies. Alternatively, after all data have been collected, students could work on the problem of finding the total number of pockets.

Continued on next page

Graphing Pocket Data   Complete the activity using the Variation, Finding the Most Common Number of Pockets. Leave students' cube trains intact. Each student then creates a representation of the day's pocket data. Provide a variety of materials, including stick-on notes, stickers or paper squares, markers and crayons, drawing paper, and graph paper for students to use.

These cube trains represent how many pockets people are wearing today. Suppose you want to show our pocket data to your family, friends, or students in another classroom or even at a different school. How could you show our pocket data on paper so that someone else could see what we found out about our pockets today?

By creating their own representations, students become more familiar with the data and may begin to develop theories as they consider how to communicate what they know about the data to an audience. Students' representations may not be precise; what's important is that the representations enable them to describe and interpret their data.

Comparing Pocket Data with Another Class
Arrange to compare pocket data with a fourth or fifth grade class. Present the following question to the students:

Do you think fifth grade students wear more, fewer, or about the same number of pockets as second grade students? Why?

Discuss students' thinking. Then investigate this question by comparing your data with data from another classroom. One way to do this is to invite the other class to participate in your Pocket Day. Do the activity first with the second graders, recording how many people have each number of pockets on the Pocket Data Chart and finding the total number of pockets. Repeat with the other students, recording their data on chart paper. Then compare the two sets of data.

How does the number of pockets in the fifth grade compare to the number of pockets in second grade? Why?

Discuss students' ideas.

Calculate the Total Number of Pockets   Divide students into groups of four or five. Each group determines the total number of pockets being worn by the group. Data from each small group are shared and recorded on the board. Using this information, students work in pairs to determine the total number of pockets worn by the class. As a group, they share strategies used for determining the total number of pockets.

In another variation, students share individual pocket data with the group. Each student records this information using a class list of names to keep track. They then determine the total number of pockets worn by the students in the class. Observe how students calculate the total number of pockets. What materials do they use? Do they group familiar numbers together, such as combinations of 10, doubles, or multiples of 5?

Time and Time Again

Time and Time Again is one of the classroom routines included in the grade 2 *Investigations* curriculum. This routine helps second graders develop an understanding of time-related ideas such as sequencing of events, the passage of time, duration of time periods, and identifying important times in their day.

Because many of the ideas and suggestions presented in this routine will be incorporated throughout the school day and into other parts of the curriculum, we encourage teachers to use this routine in whatever way meets the needs of their students and their classroom. We believe that learning about time and understanding ideas about time happen best when activities are presented *over* time and have relevance to students' experiences and lives.

Daily Schedule Post a daily schedule. Identify important times (start of school, math, music, recess, reading) using both analog (clockface) and digital (10:15) representation. Discuss the daily schedule each day and encourage students to compare the actual starting time of, say, math class with what is posted on the schedule.

Talk Time Identify times as you talk with students. For example, "In 15 minutes we will be cleaning up and going to recess." Include specific times and refer to a clock in your classroom, "It's now 10:15. In 15 minutes we will be cleaning up and going out to recess. That will be at 10:30."

Timing One Hour Set a timer to go off at one hour intervals. Choose a starting time and write both the analog time (using a clockface) and the digital time. When the timer rings, record the time using analog and digital times. At the end of the day, students make observations about the data collected. Initially you'll want to use whole and half hours as your starting points. Gradually you can use times that are 10 or 20 minutes after the hour and also appoint students to be in charge of the timer and of recording the times.

Timing Other Intervals Set a timer to go off at 15-minute intervals over a period of two hours. Begin at the hour and, after the data have been collected, discuss with students what happened each time 15 minutes was added to the time (11:00, 11:15, 11:30, 11:45). You can also try this with 10-minute intervals.

Home Schedule Students make a schedule of important times at home. They can do this both for school days and for nonschool days. They should include both analog and digital times on their schedules. Later in the year, they can use this schedule to see if they were really on time for things like dinner, piano lessons, or bedtime. They record the actual time that events happened and calculate how early or late they were. Students can also illustrate their schedules.

Comparing Schedules Partners compare important times in their day, such as what time they eat dinner, go to bed, get up, leave for school. They can compare whether events are earlier or later, and some students might want to calculate how much earlier or later these events occur.

Life Line Students create a timeline of their life. They interview family members and collect information about important developmental milestones such as learning to walk, first word, first day of school, first lost tooth, and important family events. Students then record these events on a lifeline that is a representation of the first 7 or 8 years of their life.

Clock Data Students collect data about the types of clocks they have in their home—digital or analog. They make a representation of these data and as a class compare their results.

- **Are there more digital or analog clocks in your house?**

- **Is this true of our class set of data?**

- **How could we compare our individual data to a class set of data?**

Continued on next page

Time Collection   Students bring in things from home that have to do with time. Include digital and analog clocks as well as timers of various sorts. These items could be sorted and grouped in different ways. Some students may be interested in investigating different types of time pieces such as sundials, sand timers, and pendulums.

How Long Is a Minute?   As you time 1 minute, students close their eyes and then raise their hands when they think a minute has gone by. Ask, "Is a minute longer or shorter than you imagined?" Repeat this activity or have students do this with partners.

What Can You Do in a Minute?   When students are familiar with timing 1 minute, they can work in pairs and collect data about things they can do in 1 minute. Brainstorm a list of events that students might try. Some ideas second graders have suggested include: writing their name, doing jumping jacks or sit-ups, hopping on one foot, saying the ABC's, snapping together interlocking cubes, writing certain numbers or letters (this is great practice for working on reversals!), and drawing geometric shapes such as triangles, squares, or stars. Each student chooses four or five activities to do in 1 minute. Before they collect the data, they predict how many they can do. Then with partners they gather the data and compare.

How Long Does It Take?   Using a stopwatch or a clock with a second hand, time how long it takes students to complete certain tasks such as lining up, giving out supplies, or cleaning up after math time. Emphasize doing these things in a responsible way. Students can take turns being "timekeepers."

Stopwatches   Most second graders are fascinated by stopwatches. You will find that students come up with many ideas about what to time. If possible, acquire a stopwatch for your classroom. (Inexpensive ones are available through educational supply catalogs.) Having stopwatches available in the classroom allows students to teach each other about time and to keep track of time.

The following activities will help ensure that this unit is comprehensible to students who are acquiring English as a second language. The suggested approach is based on *The Natural Approach: Language Acquisition in the Classroom* by Stephen D. Krashen and Tracy D. Terrell (Alemany Press, 1983). The intent is for second-language learners to acquire new vocabulary in an active, meaningful context.

Note that *acquiring* a word is different from *learning* a word. Depending on their level of proficiency, students may be able to comprehend a word upon hearing it during an investigation, without being able to say it. Other students may be able to use the word orally but not read or write it. The goal is to help students naturally acquire targeted vocabulary at their present level of proficiency.

We suggest using these activities just before the related investigations. The activities can be led by English-proficient students.

Investigation 4

more, fewer

1. Draw a circle and a square. Put 5 dots inside the circle and 8 dots inside the square. Lead students in counting aloud as you point to each dot in the circle. Do the same for the square.

2. Ask students if there are more dots inside the square or inside the circle. Explain that to answer the question, you can compare the dots. **There are *more* dots inside the square than inside the circle, or there are *fewer* dots inside the circle than inside the square.**

3. Next, put 6 dots inside a circle and 3 dots inside a square. Ask questions that compare the number of dots inside the shapes, emphasizing the language of comparing. **Does the circle have *more* or *fewer* dots than the square? Does the square have *more* or *fewer* dots than the circle?**

4. Give students paper and pencil. Ask them to draw a circle and a square (large enough for them to draw dots inside). Give oral directions for putting dots inside the shapes.

   Put more dots in the circle than in the square.

   Put fewer dots in the square than in the circle.

   Put four more dots in the square than in the circle.

   After each direction, encourage students to describe what they drew (for example, "I put 5 dots in the circle and 3 dots in the square. 5 is more than 3").

Investigation 5

similar, same, different

1. Ask two or three students who are wearing something similar or who have a similar attribute to stand where the rest of the group can see them. (For example, students may be wearing jeans, wearing stripes, wearing glasses, or have dark hair.) Lead students in recognizing the similar attribute by asking questions. **Is Ayaz wearing jeans? Is Ping wearing jeans? What is the *same* about these students?**

2. Ask another student with the same attribute to join the group. Ask questions leading the students to make visual comparisons. **Is Juanita wearing something the *same as* (or *similar to*) the rest of the group? What is it?**

3. Have a student who does not share the attribute stand near the others. Encourage the group to compare this student with those already standing, and decide if he or she shares a similar attribute. Help students describe their observations. (For example, "Graham is wearing white shorts. His shorts are *different* from the jeans that Ayaz and Ping are wearing.")

4. Challenge students to identify two class members that share the *same* attribute and two class members with a *different* attribute. Students can describe what they found for the rest of the group.

Teacher Tutorial

Contents

Overview

The units in *Investigations in Number, Data, and Space®* ask teachers to think in new ways about mathematics and how students best learn math. Units such as *Mathematical Thinking* add another challenge for teachers—to think about how computers might support and enhance mathematical learning. Before you can think about how computers might support learning in your classroom, you need to know what the computer component is, how it works, and how it is designed to be used in the unit. This Tutorial is included to help you learn these things.

The Tutorial is written for you as an adult learner, as a mathematical explorer, as an educational researcher, as a curriculum designer, and finally—putting all these together—as a classroom teacher. Although it includes parallel (and in some cases the same) investigations as the unit, it is not intended as a walk-through of the student activities in the unit. Rather, it is meant to provide experience using the computer program *Shapes* and to familiarize you with some of the mathematical thinking in the unit.

The Tutorial is organized in sessions parallel to the unit. Included in each session are detailed step-by-step instructions for how to use the computer and the *Shapes* program, along with suggestions for exploring more deeply. The later parts of the Tutorial include more detail about each component of *Shapes* and can be used for reference. There is also detailed help available in the *Shapes* program itself.

Shapes is a computer manipulative, a software version of pattern blocks and tangrams, that extends what students can do with these shapes. Students create as many copies of each shape as they want and use computer tools to move, combine, and duplicate these shapes to make pictures and designs and to solve problems.

Teachers new to using computers and *Shapes* can follow the detailed step-by-step instructions. Those with more experience might not need to read each step. As is true with learning any new approach or tool, you will test out hypotheses, make mistakes, be temporarily stumped, go down wrong paths, and so on. This is part of learning but may be doubly frustrating because you are dealing with computers. It might be helpful to work through the Tutorial and the unit in parallel with another teacher. If you get particularly frustrated, ask for help from the school computer coordinator or another teacher more familiar with using computers. It is not necessary to complete the Tutorial before beginning to teach the unit. You can work through in parts, as you prepare for parallel investigations in the unit.

Although the Tutorial will help prepare you for teaching the unit, you will learn most about *Shapes* and how it supports the unit as you work side by side with your students.

About *Shapes*

Shapes is a computer manipulative, a software version of pattern blocks and tangrams, that extends what students can do with these shapes. Students create as many copies of each shape as they want and use computer tools to move, combine, and duplicate these shapes to make pictures and designs and to solve problems.

What Should I Read First?

Read the next section, Starting *Shapes*, for specific information on how to load the *Shapes* program and choose an activity.

The section Free Explore takes you step by step through an example of working with *Shapes*. Read this section for a sense of what the program can do.

The section Using *Shapes* provides detailed information about each aspect of *Shapes*. Read this to learn *Shapes* thoroughly or to answer specific questions.

Starting *Shapes*

Note: These directions assume that *Shapes* has been installed on the hard drive of your computer. If not, see How to Install *Shapes* on Your Computer, p. 169.

☞ 1. Turn on the computer by doing the following:

   a. If you are using an electrical power surge protector, switch to the ON position.

   b. Switch the computer (and the monitor, if separate) to the ON position.

   c. Wait until the desktop or workspace appears.

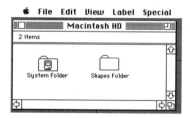

☞ 2. Open *Shapes* by doing the following:

   a. Double-click on the *Shapes* Folder icon if it is not already open. To double-click, click twice in rapid succession without moving the pointer.

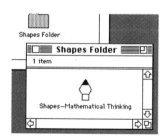

   b. Double-click on the *Shapes* icon in this folder.

Shapes—Mathematical Thinking

c. Wait until the *Shapes* opening screen appears. Click on the bar "Click on this window to continue." when the message appears.

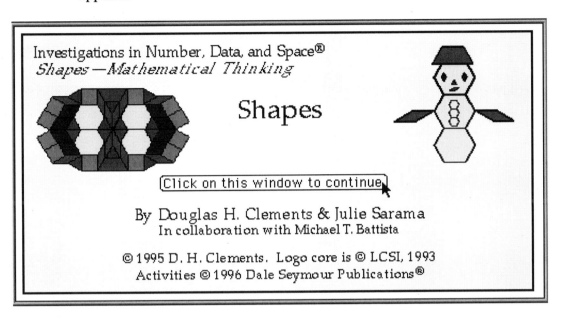

Start an activity by doing the following:

Click on Free Explore (or any activity you want).

How to Start an Activity

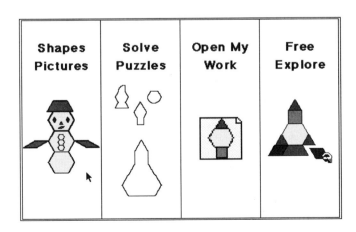

When you choose an activity, the Tool bar, Shape bar, and Work window fill the screen.

The following section provides a step-by-step example of working with *Shapes*.

About Free Explore

The Free Explore activity is available for you to use as an environment to explore *Shapes*. It can also be used to extend and enhance activities.

When you choose Free Explore, you begin with an empty Work window. You can build a picture in that window with the shapes from the Shape bar. The tools in the Tool bar enable you to move, duplicate, and glue the shapes you select from the Work window.

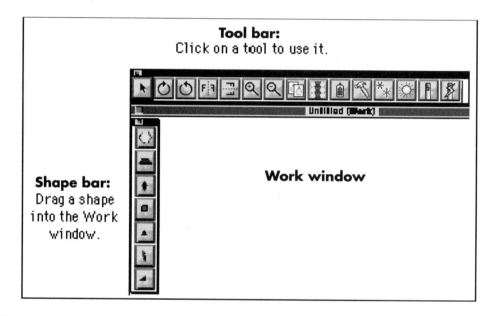

Tool bar:
Click on a tool to use it.

Untitled (Work)

Shape bar:
Drag a shape into the Work window.

Work window

Building a Picture

Let's begin by making a building in the Work window.

☛ 1. Build the front of the building by doing the following:

a. Drag an orange square shape off the Shape bar.

Move the cursor so it is on the square. It becomes a hand.	Click the mouse button and hold it down . . .	. . . while you move the square where you want it.

b. Slide the square to the middle of the Work window.

If you need to move the square, just click on it and drag it again.

c. Drag another orange square shape from the Shape bar and place it next to the first one.

Notice that the new square "snaps" right next to the first one.

d. Continue this procedure until the "front" of the building is finished.

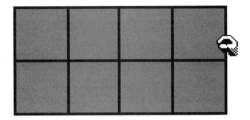

☞ **2.** Build the side of the building by doing the following:

Drag two tan rhombuses (thin diamonds) for the side of the building from the Shape bar and slide into place.

Young students might not do this, but we're going to try for a 3-dimensional effect!

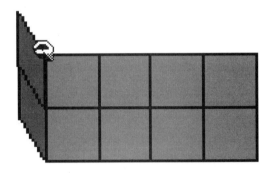

☞ **3.** Start the roof of the building by doing the following:

Drag a blue rhombus (diamond) from the Shape bar.

This shape will have to be turned to make it fit.

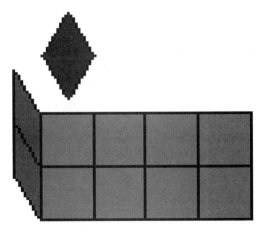

☞ **4.** Turn the blue rhombus by doing the following:

a. Click on the Left Turn tool in the Tool bar.

The cursor changes from an arrow to a left-turn circle.

b. Click this new cursor on the blue rhombus.
The rhombus turns to the left.

c. Click on the blue rhombus a second time.
The rhombus turns to the left again, and it is ready to be slid into place.

☞ **5.** Slide the blue rhombus into place by doing the following:

a. Click on the Arrow tool in the Tool bar.
The cursor changes back to an arrow.

b. Slide the rhombus into place.

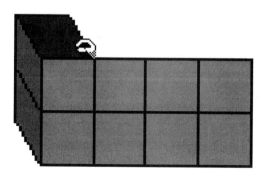

6. Duplicate the blue rhombus three times to make three copies of it:

a. Click on the Duplicate tool in the Tool bar.

The cursor changes from an arrow to the Duplicate icon .

b. Click the Duplicate tool *on* the blue rhombus.

A duplicate is made. Using the Duplicate tool is particularly appropriate in this case because the duplicate is turned the correct way automatically.

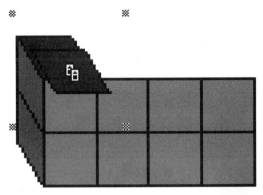

c. Click on the Arrow tool in the Tool bar.

The cursor changes back to an arrow.

d. Slide the duplicate rhombus into place.

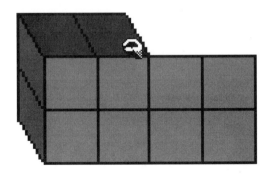

e. Repeat steps a. to d. to make and position two more duplicates.

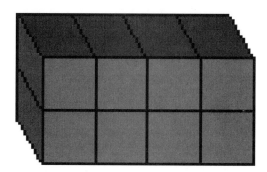

Note: To be more efficient, we could have duplicated three copies right away and then slid each into place one after the other.

☞ **7.** Make a half-circle doorway.

a. Drag a quarter circle from the Shape bar. Slide it into place.

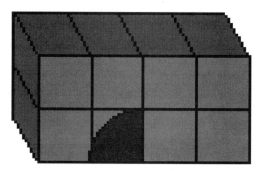

b. Drag another quarter circle (or duplicate the first one) and slide it into place.

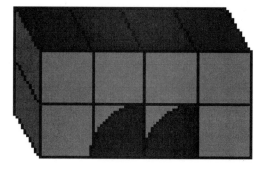

c. Click on the Vertical Flip tool in the Tool bar.

The cursor changes from an arrow to the Vertical Flip icon **F⅂**.

d. Click the Vertical Flip tool on the second quarter circle.

The shape flips over a vertical line through the center of the shape. Because the quarter circle is symmetric, we could have also turned it several times to the right, but flipping is more efficient.

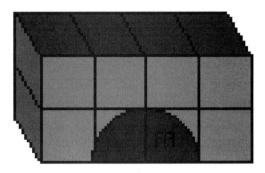

Our building is finished.

---

 1. Make a sun.

a. Drag a yellow hexagon from the Shape bar.

Place it in the upper right-hand corner of the Work window.

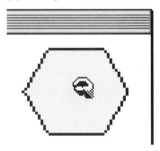

b. Get another yellow hexagon and place it right over the first one.

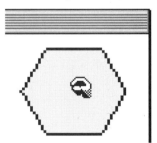

c. Click on the Right Turn tool in the Tool bar.

The cursor changes from an arrow to the Right Turn icon ↻.

More About Building Pictures

d. Click the Right Turn tool on the second hexagon.

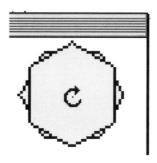

Our sun is finished. Now let's add a walkway. It will be a pattern of several shapes. First, we'll design the unit.

 1. Make a unit for the walkway.

    a. Drag a yellow hexagon, a red trapezoid, a green triangle, and a blue rhombus from the Shape bar.

    Place the shapes in the lower left-hand corner of the Work window as shown. Some shapes will have to be turned to make the pattern shown.

    b. Click on the Glue tool in the Tool bar.

    The cursor changes from an arrow to the Glue icon 🔲.

    c. Click in the middle of *each* of the four shapes in the unit.

    The cursor changes to a "squirt glue" icon whenever you click on a shape that has not yet been glued. Note that you have to click on each shape; even though they are "snapped" and touching sides, you must indicate each one you want glued together by clicking in the middle of each shape.

    The four shapes are now a glued group. They can be moved, turned, flipped, or duplicated as if they were one shape.

You can check that the shapes are one glued group. Move the cursor to the Glue tool in the Tool bar and hold down the mouse button. The following will appear on your screen, indicating one group.

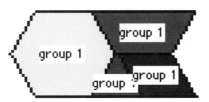

☞ 2. Duplicate the unit for the walkway.

a. Click on the Duplicate tool in the Tool bar.

The cursor changes from an arrow to the Duplicate icon ⊞.

b. Click the Duplicate tool on the blue rhombus.
A duplicate is made. Using the Duplicate tool is necessary because we're going to make a repeating pattern.

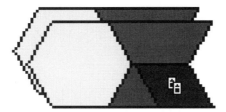

☞ 3. Define the motion for the pattern.

a. Click on the Arrow tool in the Tool bar.
The cursor changes back to an arrow.

b. Slide the duplicate of the unit where you want it to be for the start of the pattern.

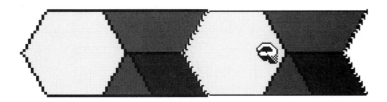

☞ 4. Continue the pattern.

    a. Click on the Pattern button in the Tool bar.

       The Pattern tool is a button. Simply clicking on a button will perform the action immediately. The next part of the pattern is put into place.

    b. Keep clicking on the Pattern button until your walkway extends across the window.

Our walkway is finished. Now let's make trees. Use the Pattern tool again to make the top of the first tree.

☞ 1. Make a unit for the treetop.

    Get a green triangle from the Shape bar.

    Place it on the left-hand side of the Work window. We don't need to glue this time because our unit is just one shape.

☞ 2. Duplicate it.

    a. Click on the Duplicate tool in the Tool bar.

       The cursor changes from an arrow to the Duplicate icon .

    b. Click the Duplicate tool on the triangle.

☞ 3. Define the motion for the pattern.

    a. Click on the Right Turn tool in the Tool bar.

       The cursor changes back to the Right Turn icon .

    b. Turn the duplicate of the unit to the right two times.

c. Click on the Arrow tool in the Tool bar.
The cursor changes back to an arrow.

d. Slide the duplicate of the unit where you want it to be for the start of the pattern.

We have now defined the motion for the pattern.

☛ **4.** Continue the pattern.

a. Click on the Pattern button in the Tool bar four times to

complete the treetop.

We'll finish the tree.

☞ 1. Make a trunk and ground cover.

    a. Drag two squares from the Shape bar.
Place the squares below the green
triangles as shown.

    b. Drag three tan rhombuses from the Shape bar. Turn them left
three times and place them as ground cover. (You could also get
one, turn it left three times, then use the Duplicate tool to make
two copies.)

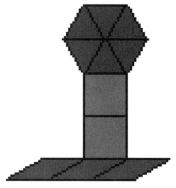

We need ground cover in back of the tree too.

    c. Drag three more tan rhombuses from the Shape bar. Place them
in "back" of the others. (You could use the Duplicate tool to do
this.)

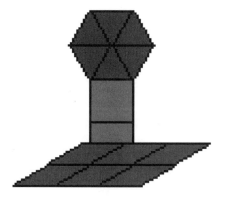

The tree shouldn't be behind the ground cover.

☞ 2. Bring the tree trunk to the front of the ground cover.

    a. Select the bottom orange square by clicking in the middle of it one time.

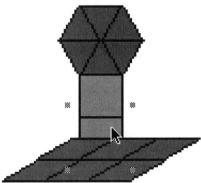

    The small gray "selection" squares show that the bottom orange square is "selected." You can choose menu items to apply to selected shapes.

    b. Choose **Bring To Front** from the **Edit** menu.

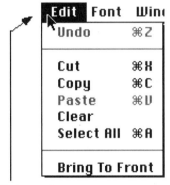

Point to the menu you want and press the mouse button . . .

. . . then move the cursor to **Bring To Front**

    The orange square is brought to the front of the picture.

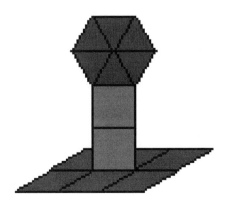

☞ **3.** Glue the tree and ground cover together.

In Step 2, you selected a single shape, the orange square, and applied the action (**Bring To Front**) to it. You can also select a *group* of shapes and apply a tool or action to the entire group at one time. This will make gluing all these shapes together easier.

a. Place the arrow at the top left corner of the group of shapes in the tree.

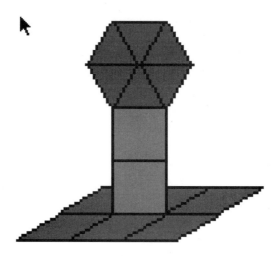

b. Drag diagonally to enclose the shapes in a dotted rectangle . . .

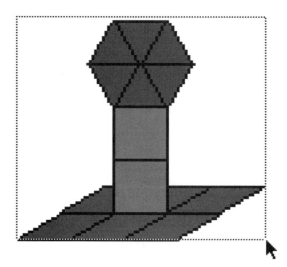

c. ... and release the mouse button.

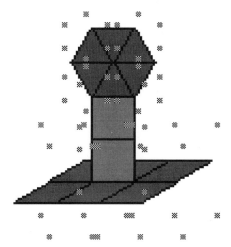

d. Use the Glue tool to glue all the shapes into a group at once by clicking in the middle of any one of them.

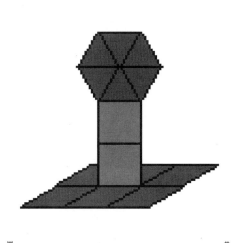

Click on the Arrow tool in the Tool bar. Now the small gray "selection" squares will surround a whole group instead of each individual shape.

You can now do something to all these shapes at once: duplicate them, slide them, turn them, or flip them as one shape. Note that if you click on one of the selected group and slide the whole group, there may be a delay while the *Shapes* program builds an outline of the group.

Next let's try duplicating a group.

☞ 1. Duplicate the tree.

Use the Duplicate tool to make several copies of the tree and place them where you like.

☞ 2. Add any finishing touches.

In the picture below, blue rhombuses connecting the building and the walkway were added, some shapes were moved, and the **Bring To Front** command was applied to add a few finishing touches.

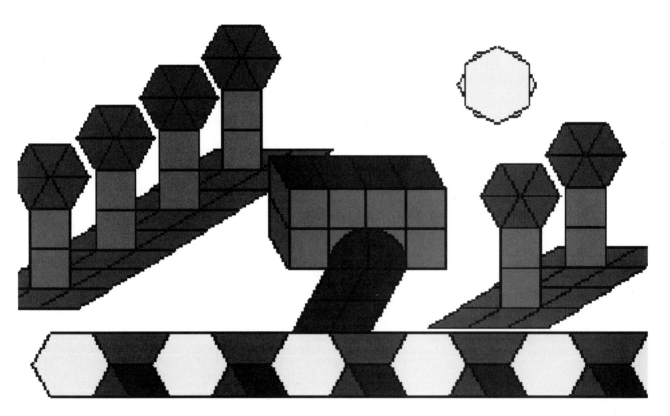

The picture is finished.

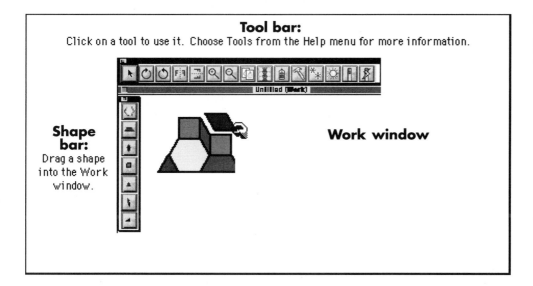

Tool bar:
Click on a tool to use it. Choose Tools from the Help menu for more information.

Untitled (Work)

Shape bar:
Drag a shape into the Work window.

Work window

Begin by dragging a shape from the Shape bar (the vertical, "floating" bar on the left) to the Work window (the large blank window). Dragging means clicking on a shape and then holding the mouse button down while you move the mouse.

Move the cursor to a shape with the mouse. It becomes a hand.	Click the mouse button and hold it down . . .	. . . while you move the new shape where you want it.

Once the shape is placed in the Work window, you can slide it again by dragging it with the Arrow tool. If you place one shape so that one of its sides is close to a side of another shape, the two shapes will "snap" together.

You can change the position of the shape, or duplicate it, by using the tools in the Tool bar. The tool that is "active," or in use, is surrounded by a black outline (like the arrow tool shown in the diagram on p. 156). Another way to see which tool is active is by the shape of the cursor.

Only the most commonly used tools are available and displayed for each activity. All tools are available for Free Explore.

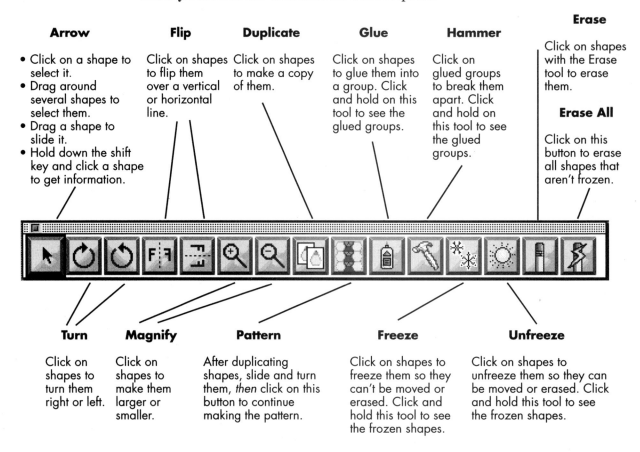

Arrow
- Click on a shape to select it.
- Drag around several shapes to select them.
- Drag a shape to slide it.
- Hold down the shift key and click a shape to get information.

Flip
Click on shapes to flip them over a vertical or horizontal line.

Duplicate
Click on shapes to make a copy of them.

Glue
Click on shapes to glue them into a group. Click and hold on this tool to see the glued groups.

Hammer
Click on glued groups to break them apart. Click and hold on this tool to see the glued groups.

Erase
Click on shapes with the Erase tool to erase them.

Erase All
Click on this button to erase all shapes that aren't frozen.

Turn
Click on shapes to turn them right or left.

Magnify
Click on shapes to make them larger or smaller.

Pattern
After duplicating shapes, slide and turn them, *then* click on this button to continue making the pattern.

Freeze
Click on shapes to freeze them so they can't be moved or erased. Click and hold this tool to see the frozen shapes.

Unfreeze
Click on shapes to unfreeze them so they can be moved or erased. Click and hold this tool to see the frozen shapes.

To use most tools (except Pattern and Erase All, which are buttons):

☞ 1. Click on a tool in the Tool bar to make it active. The cursor will change to look like the tool.

☞ 2. Click in the middle of a shape to perform the action. If you click one of several shapes that are "selected," the action is performed on each of the selected shapes. See the following section, The Arrow Tool, for more information about selecting shapes.

Pattern and Erase All are **buttons**. Simply clicking on a button will perform the action immediately.

The following sections discuss the tools in more detail.

With the Arrow tool, you can drag shapes to slide them. This is the most important use of the Arrow tool.

1. Click in the middle of a shape and hold the mouse button down . . .

2. . . . while you move the mouse, sliding the shape.

3. Release the button to stop sliding.

You can also select shapes with the Arrow tool.

Note: You can do most tasks in *Shapes*, including sliding, without ever selecting shapes. It's usually just a convenience for taking some action on several shapes at once. Before we discuss how to select shapes, let's describe what "selecting" means.

Selected shapes are shown surrounded with small gray squares.

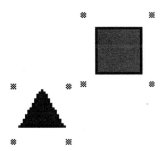

Selected shapes can be copied to the clipboard (a place in computer memory for temporary, invisible storage) or cut—copied to the clipboard *and* removed from the Work window—using commands on the **Edit** menu. Also, if you apply a tool to one shape that is part of a group of selected shapes, the tool will automatically be applied to each shape in the group.

There are two ways to select shapes. First, you can click on any shape with the Arrow tool. That selects the shape. (If it is *already* selected, this will "unselect" the shape.) Second, you can select multiple shapes that are near one another:

1. Place the arrow at one corner of the group of shapes. Press the mouse button.

2. Drag diagonally to enclose the shapes in a dotted rectangle . . .

3. . . . and release the mouse button.

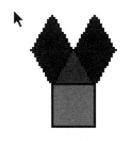

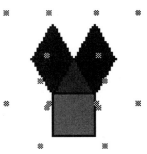

Now you can do something to all these shapes at once, for example, copy or cut them, slide them all together, or flip them all. Note that if you click on one of the selected group and slide the whole group, there may be a delay while the *Shapes* program builds an outline. Hold the mouse button down without moving the mouse until the outline appears.

You can use the Arrow tool to shift-click on a shape to get information about it. To shift-click, hold the shift key down while clicking on a shape. Click again to clear the message.

I am a frozen square in group 1

One final feature: if you're using any other tool and you want to use the Arrow tool for a quick selection or slide, just hold down the Command ♥ key. *Shapes* will know to use the Arrow tool while the Command key is held down. When you let go of the Command key, *Shapes* will return to the previous tool.

Turn, Flip, and Magnifying Tools: Moving and Sizing

You can use these tools to turn or flip shapes:

One shape: Click on a shape with the tool. For example, if you click on the shape with the first flip tool, the shape flips over a vertical line through the center of the shape.

Several shapes: After the shapes have been selected, click on one of them with the tool. For example, if you click on one with the first Turn tool, each shape turns right around its center.

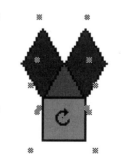

To magnify shapes: If you click on a shape with the first Magnify tool, the shape gets bigger. The second Magnify tool will make it smaller. Shapes that are different sizes will not snap to each other.

You can use the Glue tool to glue several shapes together into a group. This group is a new shape you have created. You can slide, turn, and flip it as a unit—that is, as if it were a single shape. For example, you can glue several shapes and then move them or duplicate them.

Glue and Hammer Tools: Combining and Breaking Apart

To use the Glue tool,

☞ 1. Click on the Glue tool in the Tool bar to make it active.

☞ 2. Click on each shape you wish to glue together into a group.

   If there are only two shapes, or if two or more shapes are "snapped" or touching, you still have to click on each of them. Click in the middle of each shape and the computer glues them together. Similarly, if you select a group of shapes, and click on one shape, the group will be glued.

   You can add more shapes to an already glued group. Click on one shape in the glued group, then click on one shape in the new group. The two groups will now be glued.

☞ 3. Click on the Arrow tool or any other tool. All the shapes you glued will become a single, new group.

The small gray "selection" squares will surround a whole group instead of each individual shape.

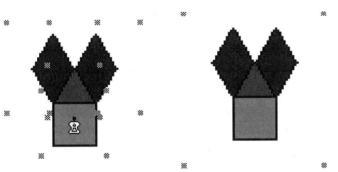

The group will now act as a single unit. For example, if you click on the group with the Right Turn tool, the group turns *as one shape* around the center of the group.

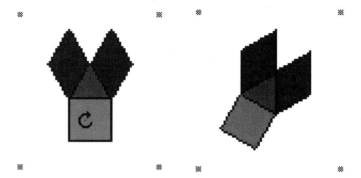

What if you want to make two separate groups? Suppose you made two different kinds of houses and you want each to be glued in a different group. You can't glue all the shapes in each of the houses at once; that would make one two-house group. Instead, you must glue one house, clicking on the Arrow tool to end the gluing process and glue that group. Then you must choose the Glue tool again and glue the second house.

Sometimes it helps to know what shapes are already glued into groups. Hold the mouse button down on either the Glue or Hammer tool on the Tool bar to see which shapes are in which groups.

☞ 1. Hold the button down on the Glue (or Hammer) tool to see the group number on each shape.

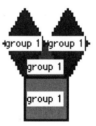

Use the Hammer tool to break apart glued shapes. Click on any shape in the group with the hammer to break apart the group.

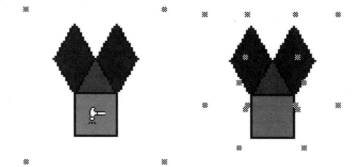

The Pattern tool is a **button**. You just click on it to perform the action (the Erase All button works the same way). To use the Pattern button, you must first make a pattern.

☞ 1. Make a basic unit for the pattern. Any shape or combination of shapes can be used as this unit. If you wish to turn the unit later to start the pattern, you must glue the shapes in the basic unit to form a group. Turn patterns must have a single glued group as the basic unit.

☞ 2. Duplicate this unit with the Duplicate tool. (You can also choose **Copy** and then **Paste** from the **Edit** menu.)

☞ 3. Move the duplicate of the unit where you want it to be for the start of the pattern by using the tools. You can slide the duplicate or turn it. (Remember, if you turn it as in this example, all the shapes in the duplicate must have been glued into one group.)

☞ 4. Now, click on the Pattern button as many times as you wish to continue the pattern. If a duplicate goes off the Work window, you will hear a beep and the Pattern button will not make any more copies.

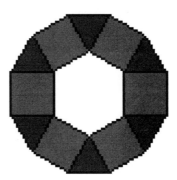

The pattern below was made by sliding the duplicate and then clicking on the Pattern button.

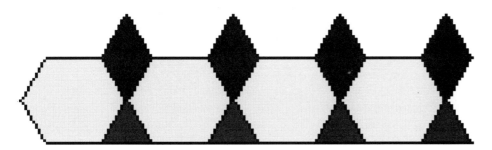

The Pattern tool makes patterns composed of slides and turns. If you want flipped shapes in your pattern, use these steps to make a basic unit (Step 1, p. 161):

    a. Glue a group.

    b. Duplicate the group.

    c. Use the Flip tool to flip the duplicate.

    d. Glue the two groups (the original and its flipped [mirror] image) together to make the basic unit for the pattern.

    e. Continue with Step 2 (p. 161).

Freeze and Unfreeze Tools: Combining and Breaking Apart

You can use the Freeze tool to "freeze" shapes. Frozen shapes can't be moved or erased. They are frozen in place (in comparison, the Glue tool glues shapes to each other; however, the glued group can still be moved).

Freezing shapes allows you to manipulate other shapes without accidentally moving or erasing those that are frozen. Click on a shape with the Unfreeze tool to unfreeze it. Click and hold either tool on the Tool bar to see the frozen shapes.

Using Menu Commands

To use any menu commands, do the following:

Point to the menu you want and press the mouse button . . .

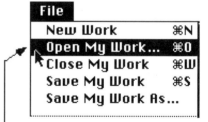

. . . then drag the selection bar to your choice and release the button.

The **File** menu deals with documents and quitting.

New Work starts a new document. The ⌘N indicates that, instead of selecting this from the menu, you could enter ⌘N or **Command N** by holding down the **Command** key (with the ⌘ and symbols on it) and then pressing the N key.

Open My Work opens previously saved work.

Close My Work closes present work.

Save My Work saves the work.

Save My Work As saves the work with a new name or to a different disk or folder.

Change Activity lets you choose a different activity.

Page Setup allows you to set up how the printer will print your work.

Print prints your work.

Quit quits *Shapes*.

When you save your work for the first time, a dialogue box opens. Type a name. You may wish to include your name or initials, your work, and the date. For the remainder of that session, you can save your work simply by selecting the **Save** menu item or pressing ⌘S (**Command S**).

To share the computer with others, save your work then choose **Close My Work**. Later, to resume your work, choose **Open My Work** and select the work you saved.

When you **Quit**, you are asked whether you wish to save your work. If you choose to save at that time (you don't have to if you just saved), the same steps are followed.

The **Edit** menu contains choices to use when editing your work.

Cut deletes the selected object and saves it to a space called the clipboard.

Copy copies the selected object on the clipboard.

Paste puts the contents of the clipboard into the Work window.

Clear deletes the selected object but does not put it on the clipboard.

Select All selects all shapes. Not only is this a fast and handy shortcut, but it also helps when some shapes are nearly or totally off the Work window.

Bring To Front puts the selected shapes "in front of" unselected shapes. That is, each new shape you create will be "in front of" the shapes already on the Work window. If you want to change this, select a shape that is in the "back," hidden by other shapes, and choose **Bring To Front**.

About Menus

File

New Work	⌘N
Open My Work...	⌘O
Close My Work	⌘W
Save My Work	⌘S
Save My Work As...	
Change Activity...	
Page Setup...	
Print...	⌘P
Quit	⌘Q

Edit

Undo	⌘Z
Cut	⌘X
Copy	⌘C
Paste	⌘V
Clear	
Select All	⌘A
Bring To Front	

The **Font** menu is used to change the appearance of text in the Show Notes window. In order for any command in the **Font** menu to be highlighted, the Show Notes command in the **Windows** menu must be open.

The first names are choices of typeface.

Size and **Style** have additional choices; pull down to select them and then to the right. See the example for **Style** shown at left. The **Size** choice works the same way.

All Large changes all text in all windows to a large-size font. This is useful for demonstrations. This selection toggles (changes back and forth) between **All Large** and **All Small**.

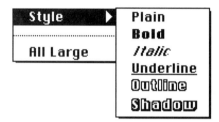

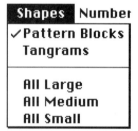

The **Windows** menu shows or hides the windows. If you hide a window such as the Tool bar, the menu item changes to **Show** followed by the name of the window—for example, **Show Tools**. You can also hide a window by clicking in the "close box" in the upper-left corner of the window.

The **Notes** Window is designed to be a word processor. Students might use this to record a strategy they used to solve a problem, or to write notes to themselves as reminders of how they plan to continue the next math session.

The **Shapes** menu contains several commands to change the shapes.

Pattern Blocks and **Tangrams** chooses one of the shape sets for the Shape bar.

All Large, **All Medium**, and **All Small** changes the size of all the shapes. Use the Magnify tools to change the size of some of the shapes. Note that shapes of different sizes do not snap to each other.

The **Number** menu is available for only certain activities that have more than one task. Select a number off the submenu to work on that number task.

Number
✓ Number 1
Number 2
Number 3
Number 4
Number 5
Number 6
Number 7
Number 8
Number 9
Number 10

The **Options** menu allows you to customize *Shapes*.

Vertical Mirror and **Horizontal Mirror** toggle (turn on and off) the Work windows mirrors, which reflect any action you take.

Snap toggles the "snap" feature, in which shapes, when moved, automatically "snap" or move next to, any other shape they are close to. You may want to turn that feature off if you have lots of shapes on the Work window, or if you are copying many shapes. This feature can slow down moving the shapes. You can turn it off temporarily to speed things up.

Options Help
Vertical Mirror
Horizontal Mirror
✓ Snap

The **Help** menu provides assistance.

Windows provides information on the three main windows: the Tool bar, the Shape bar, and the Work window.

Tools provides information on tools (represented on the Tool bar as icons, or pictures).

Directions provides instructions for the present activity.

Hints gives a series of hints on the present activity, one at a time. It is dimmed when there are no available hints.

Help
Windows...
Tools...
Directions... ⌘D
Hints... ⌘H

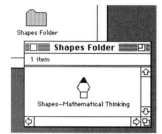

This section contains suggestions for how to correct errors and what to do in some troubling situations.

If you are new to using the computer, you might also ask a computer coordinator or an experienced friend for help.

No *Shapes* Icon to Open

- Check that *Shapes* has been installed on your computer by looking at a listing of the hard disk.
- Open the folder labeled *Shapes* by double-clicking on it.
- Find the icon for the *Shapes* application and double-click on it.

Shapes—Mathematical Thinking

Nothing Happened After Double-Clicking on the *Shapes* Icon

- If you are sure you double-clicked correctly, wait a bit longer. *Shapes* takes a while to open or load and nothing new will appear on the screen for a few seconds.
- On the other hand, you may have double-clicked too slowly, or moved the mouse between your clicks. In that case, try again.

In the Wrong Activity

- Choose **Change Activity** from the **File** menu.

A Window Closed by Mistake

- Choose **Show Window** from the **Windows** menu.

Windows or Tools Dragged to a Different Position by Mistake

- Drag the window back into place by following these steps: Place the pointer arrow in the stripes of the title bar. Press and hold the button as you move the mouse. An outline of the window indicates the new location. Release the button and the window moves to that location.

I Clicked Somewhere and Now *Shapes* Is Gone! What Happened?

You probably clicked in a part of the screen not used by *Shapes* and the computer therefore took you to another application, such as the "desktop."

- Click on a *Shapes* window, if visible.
- Double-click on the *Shapes* program icon.

How Do I Select a Section of Text?

In certain situations, you may wish to copy or delete a section or block of text.

- Point and click at one end of the text. Drag the mouse by holding down the mouse button as you move to the other end of the text. Release the mouse button. Then use the **Edit** menu to **Copy**, **Cut**, and **Paste**.

System Error Message

Some difficulty with the *Shapes* program or your computer caused the computer to stop functioning.

- Turn off the computer and repeat the steps to turn it on and start *Shapes* again. Any work that you saved will still be available to open from your disk.

I Tried to Print and Nothing Happened

- Check that the printer is connected and turned on.
- When printers are not functioning properly, a system error may occur, causing the computer to "freeze." If there is no response from the keyboard or when moving or clicking with the mouse, you may have to turn off the computer and start over.

I Printed the Work Window but Not Everything Printed

- Choose the Color/Grayscale option for printing.
- If your printer has no such option (e.g., an older black and white printer), you need to find a different printer to print graphics in color.

If the *Shapes* program does not understand a command or has a suggestion, a dialogue box may appear with one of the following messages. Read the message, click on **[OK]** or press **<return>** from the keyboard, and correct the situation as needed.

Disk or directory full.

The computer disk is full.

■ Use **Save My Work As** to choose a different disk.

I'm having trouble with the disk or drive.

The disk might be write-protected, there is no disk in the drive, or some similar problem.

■ Use **Save My Work As** to choose a different disk.

Out of space.

There is no free memory left in the computer.

■ Eliminate shapes you don't need.
■ Save and start new work.

How to Install *Shapes* on Your Computer

The *Shapes* disk that you received with this unit contains the *Shapes* program and a Read Me file. You may run the program directly from this disk, but it is better to put a copy of the program and the Read Me file on your hard disk and store the original disk for safekeeping. Putting a program on your hard disk is called *installing* it.

Note: *Shapes* runs on a Macintosh II computer or above, with 4 MB of internal memory (RAM) and Apple System Software 7.0 or later. (*Shapes* can run on a Macintosh with less internal memory, but the system software must be configured to use a minimum of memory.)

To install the contents of the *Shapes* disk on your hard drive, follow the instructions for your type of computer or these steps:

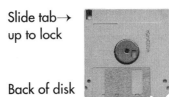

Slide tab→
up to lock

Back of disk

☞ 1. Lock the *Shapes* program disk by sliding up the black tab on the back, so the hole is open.

The *Shapes* disk is your master copy. Locking the disk allows copying while protecting its contents.

☞ 2. Insert the *Shapes* disk into the floppy disk drive.

☞ 3. Double-click on the icon of the *Shapes* disk to open it.

☞ 4. Double-click on the Read Me file to open and read it for any recent changes in how to install or use *Shapes*. Click in the close box after reading.

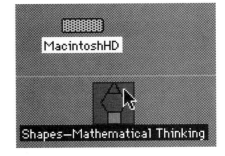

☞ 5. Click on and drag the *Shapes* disk icon (the outline moves) to the hard disk icon until the hard disk icon is highlighted, then release the mouse button.

The message appears indicating that the contents of the *Shapes* disk are being copied to the hard disk. The copy is in a folder on the hard disk with the name *Shapes*.

☞ 6. Eject the *Shapes* disk by selecting it (clicking on the icon) and choosing **Put Away** from the **File** menu. Store the disk in a safe place.

☞ 7. If the hard disk window is not open on the desktop, open the hard disk by double-clicking on the icon.

When you open the hard disk, the hard disk window appears, showing you the contents of your hard disk. It might look something like this. Among its contents is the folder labeled *Shapes* holding the contents of the *Shapes* disk.

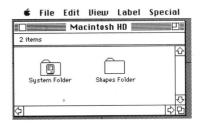

☞ 8. Double-click the *Shapes* folder to select and open it.

When you open the *Shapes* folder, the window contains the program and the Read Me file.

To select and run *Shapes,* double-click on the program icon.

Optional

For ease at startup, you might create an alias for the *Shapes* program by following these steps:

☞ 1. Select the program icon.

☞ 2. Choose **Make Alias** from the **File** menu.

The alias is connected to the original file that it represents, so that when you open an alias, you are actually opening the original file. This alias can be moved to any location on the desktop.

☞ 3. Move the *Shapes* alias out of the window to the desktop space under the hard disk icon.

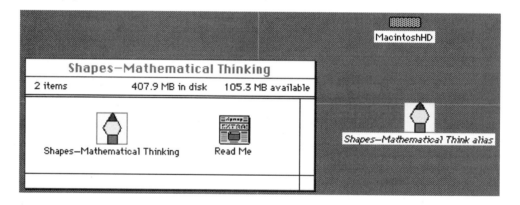

For startup, double-click on the *Shapes* alias instead of opening the *Shapes* folder to start the program inside.

Saving Work on a Different Disk

For classroom management purposes, you might want to save student work on a disk other than the program drive. Make sure that the save-to disk has been initialized (see instructions for your computer system).

☞ 1. Insert the save-to disk into the drive.

☞ 2. Choose **Save My Work As** from the **File** menu.

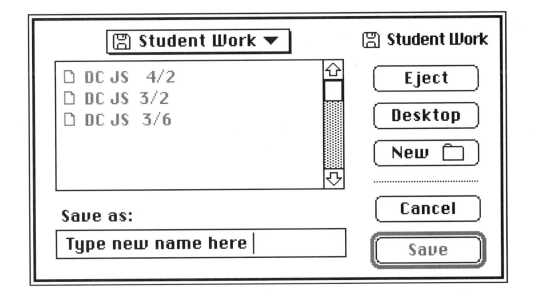

The name of the disk the computer is saving to is displayed in the dialogue box. To choose a different disk, click the **[Desktop]** button and double-click to choose and open a disk from the new menu.

☞ 3. Type a name for your work if you want to have a new or different name from the one it currently has.

☞ 4. Click on **[Save]**.

Deleting Copies of Student Work

As students no longer need previously saved work, you may want to delete their work (called "files") from a disk. This cannot be accomplished from inside the *Shapes* program. However, you can delete files from disks at any time by following directions for how to "Delete a File" for your computer system.

Blackline Masters

_____ , 19 ____

Dear Family,

We are beginning a unit called *Mathematical Thinking at Grade 2.*

The emphasis of this unit is counting and sorting. Your child will investigate every-day uses of numbers, count groups of objects in more than one way, and compare amounts. Students will play games involving money and finding different coins that show the same amount. They will explore, sort, compare, and describe different shapes. The class also will collect and organize data about themselves as a group.

Throughout this unit, your child will be using materials like interlocking cubes, pattern blocks, Geoblocks, and money. Students will be working with peers, writing and drawing about their work, and talking about how they do the problems. Each of these processes is an important emphasis in our mathematics program this year. In addition, your child will have a math folder for keeping track of the work he or she does in class.

While our class is working on this unit, you can help in several ways:

- Your child will bring home two card games, Tens Go Fish and Turn Over 10. Have your child teach family members how to play the games. Playing the games frequently will help your child learn addition combinations of 10. Please help your child find a safe place to store these materials and directions since some of them will be used repeatedly throughout the unit. An empty file folder or manila envelope might make a convenient storage place.

- As your child works on problems at home, encourage him or her to record strategies for solving problems or keeping track in ways that make sense to your child. Some children will use numbers, some will use pictures or charts, others will use words, and many will use a combination of these methods. We want all students to use problem-solving methods that are meaningful to them.

- Often children will work out number problems by using real objects. If you can, provide objects for counting, such as beans, buttons, or pennies.

- We will be taking inventories of things in the classroom, such as furniture and supplies, to count how many there are. For homework, your child will inventory something at home. This might be items in a collection or the number of windows in the house. Encourage your child to explain how the item was counted and ask if there is a way to check the count.

We are looking forward to an exciting few weeks as we create a mathematical community in our classroom.

Sincerely,

Weekly Log

Day Box

Monday, _____	
Tuesday, _____	
Wednesday, _____	
Thursday, _____	
Friday, _____	

Arranging 10 Objects

Find 10 objects that are small enough to move around, such as silverware, rocks, pennies, or sticks. Group them in different ways. Record at least two of your groupings, and write a number sentence that goes with each.

What Is Mathematics?

What is mathematics? Use words or pictures
or both to answer this question.

How Do You Use Numbers?

Find five ways that numbers are used at home. Use words or pictures to record these ways. Be sure to bring this page to school tomorrow because we will use it in class.

Ask someone at home to tell you three ways that he or she uses numbers.

Who did you ask? _____

Use words or pictures to record the three ways.

Tens Go Fish

Materials: Deck of Number Cards 0–10 (four of each) with the wild cards removed

Players: 3 to 4

How to Play

The object of the game is to get two cards that total 10.

1. Each player is dealt five cards. The rest of the cards are placed face down in the center of the table.

2. If you have any pairs of cards that total 10, put them down in front of you and replace those cards with cards from the deck.

3. Take turns. On a turn, ask <u>one</u> other player for a card that will go with a card in your hand to make 10.

4. If you get a card that makes 10, put the pair of cards down. Take one card from the deck. Your turn is over.

   If you do not get a card that makes 10, take the top card from the deck. Your turn is over.

   If the card you take from the deck makes 10 with a card in your hand, put the pair down and take another card.

5. If there are no cards left in your hand but still cards in the deck, you take two cards.

6. The game is over when there are no more cards.

7. At the end of the game, make a list of the number pairs you made.

Turn Over 10

Materials: Deck of Number Cards 0–10 (four of each) plus four wild cards

Players: 2 to 3

How to Play

The object of the game is to turn over and collect combinations of cards that total 10.

1. Arrange the cards face down in four rows of five cards. Place the rest of the deck face down in a pile.

2. Take turns. On a turn, turn over one card and then another. A wild card can be made into any number.

   If the total is less than 10, turn over another card.

   If the total is more than 10, your turn is over and the cards are turned face down in the same place.

   If the total is 10, take the cards and replace them with cards from the deck. You get another turn.

3. Place each of your card combinations of 10 in separate piles so they don't get mixed up.

4. The game is over when no more 10's can be made.

5. At the end of the game, make a list of the number combinations for 10 that you made.

Mystery Photo Recording Sheet

1. _____   2. _____

3. _____   4. _____

5. _____   6. _____

7. _____   8. _____

9. _____   10. _____

11. _____   12. _____

13. _____   14. _____

15. _____   16. _____

Cube Things

Right Hand   Left Hand   Total

_____   _____   _____

How did you figure out how many in all?

My Cube Thing is a _____.

- -

Name _____ Date _____

Cube Things

Right Hand   Left Hand   Total

_____   _____   _____

How did you figure out how many in all?

My Cube Thing is a _____.

Pockets at Home

Tell your family about Pocket Day. Find out how many pockets each person is wearing. Then figure out how many pockets your family is wearing altogether. Record your solutions using words, numbers, or pictures.

Person   Number of Pockets

_____   _____

_____   _____

_____   _____

_____   _____

If you need more lines, use the back of this page.

_____

Total number of pockets my family is wearing:

Ways to Get to _____

Write three or four stories about how to get to ____. You may illustrate your stories. Write number sentences to go with each story.

100 CHART

0	0	0	0
1	1	1	1
2	2	2	2

3	3	3	3
4	4	4	4
5	5	5	5

6	6	6	6
7	7	7	7
8	8	8	8

9	9	9	9
10	10	10	10
Wild Card	Wild Card	Wild Card	Wild Card

Card 1

Card 2

Card 3

Card 4

Card 5

Card 6

Card 7

Card 8

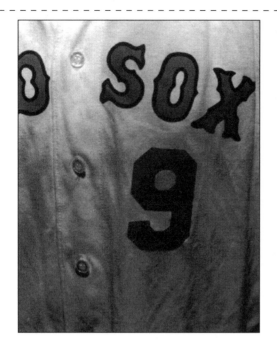

Card 9

Card 10

Card 11

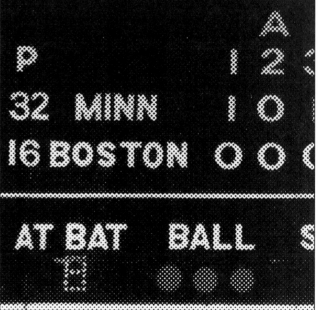

Card 12

Card 13

Card 14

Card 15

Card 16

Ways to Fill—Pattern 1

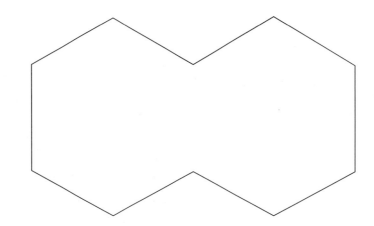

1 Shape	2 Shapes
3 Shapes	**4 Shapes**

Ways to Fill—Pattern 2

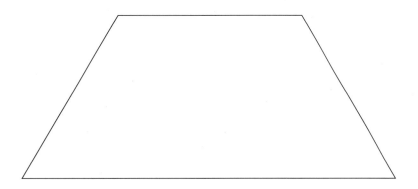

1 Shape	2 Shapes
3 Shapes	4 Shapes

Cover and Count (Shapes A–B)

Shape A

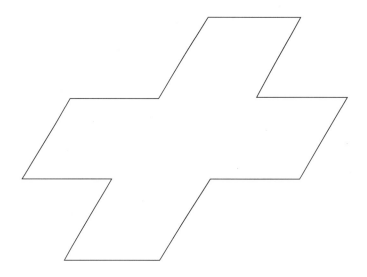

Shape B

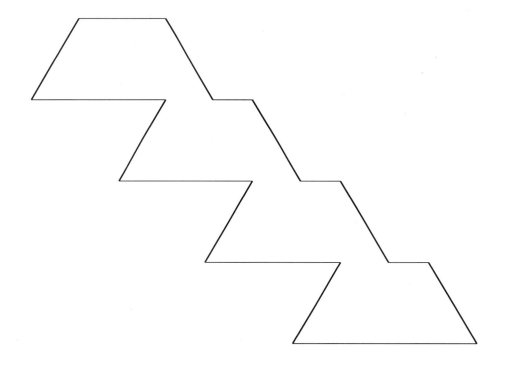

Cover and Count (Shapes C–D)

Shape C

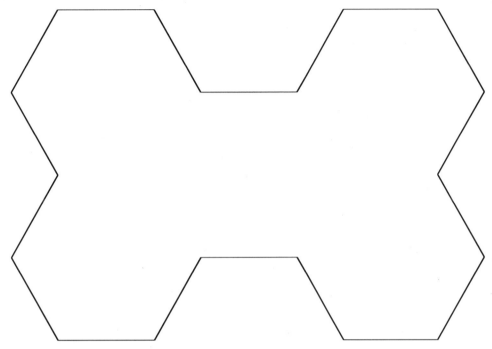

Shape D

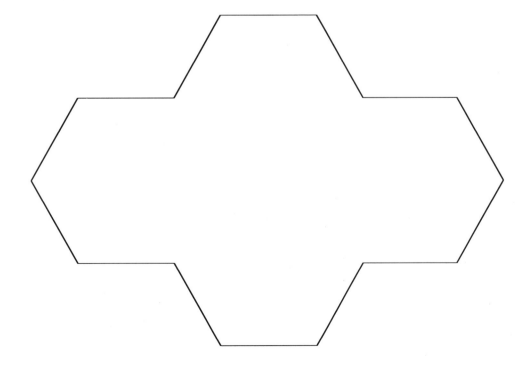

Cover and Count (Shapes E–F)

Shape E

Shape F

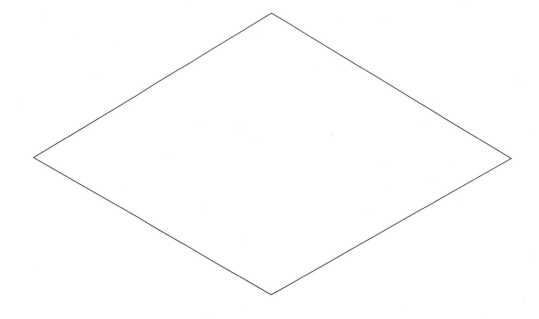

Cover and Count Recording Sheet

Shape _____

Yellow Hexagons	Red Trapezoids	Blue Rhombuses	Orange Squares	Tan Thin Rhombuses	Green Triangles	Total Blocks

Shape _____

Yellow Hexagons	Red Trapezoids	Blue Rhombuses	Orange Squares	Tan Thin Rhombuses	Green Triangles	Total Blocks

Tomorrow's Number

Make tomorrow's number _____ in at least five ways. You may ask someone else in your family to think of another way and record it here as well.

Finding Shapes

These are the pattern block shapes.

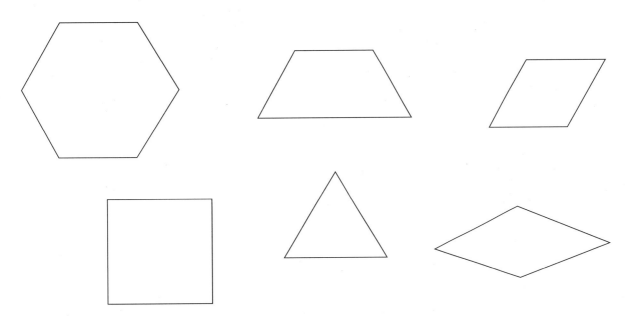

Find shapes in, around, or near your home that look like these shapes. You might find things that are exactly the same shape or things that are about the same shape.

1. Find the block.

2. Find the block.

3. Find the block.

4. Find the block.

5. Find the block.

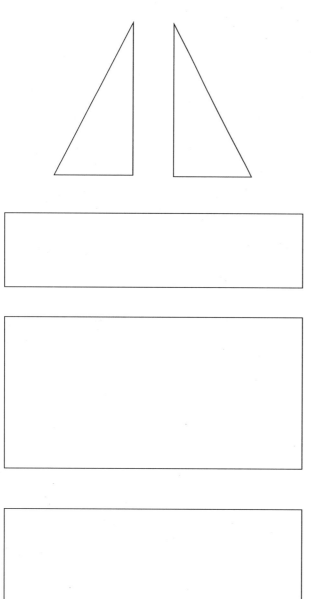

6. Find the block.

7. Find the block.

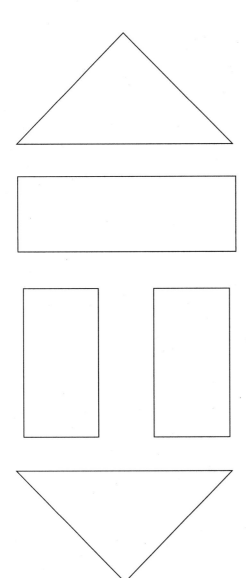

8. Find the block.

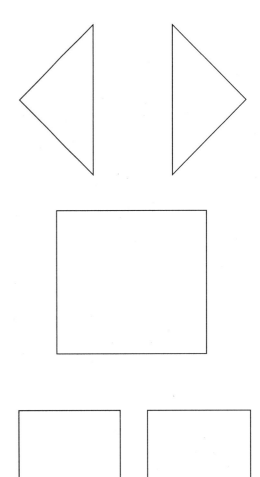

9. Find the block.

10. Find the block.

206

11. Find the block.

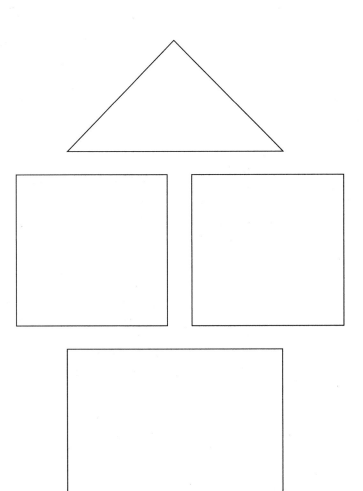

12. Find the block.

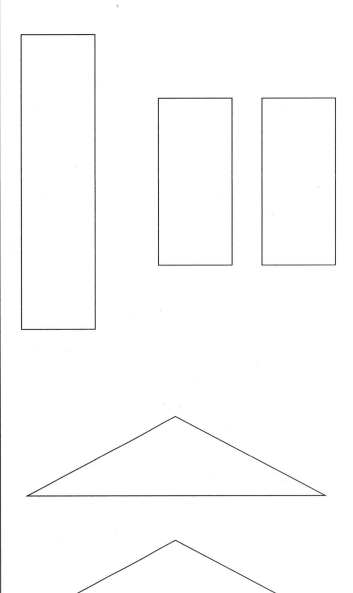

Investigation 3 • Resource
Mathematical Thinking at Grade 2

Enough for the Class?

Find how many things are in the bag.
Find a way to check your count.

Bag _____

There are _____ things in the bag.

Are there enough for the class? _____

How many leftovers will you have? _____

Explain how you figured this out.
Use numbers, words, or pictures.

Exploring Coins

Count the change in a pocket or change purse.
Record the kinds of coins here and their total value.

Is there another way you could count the coins?

If you noticed anything new about any of the coins
with someone at home, record your observations
on the back of this page.

Counting Strips

Cut these strips out and tape them together. Begin with the last number you wrote in class, and keep counting.

Tomorrow's Number Using Three Numbers

Tomorrow's number is _____. Find five ways to make tomorrow's number using three numbers. For example, $3 + 4 + 5 = 12$ is one way to use three numbers. You may use addition or subtraction.

How Many Pockets?

Imagine that five children (Ebony, Trini, Simon, Carla, and Chen) have a total of 20 pockets. How many pockets might each of these children be wearing? Find three different ways that five children might be wearing 20 pockets altogether. Show your solutions using words, numbers, or pictures.

Inventory

Category: _____

Group: _____	Group: _____
Group: _____	Group: _____
Group: _____	Group: _____

Total in category: _____

This is how I counted:

Practice Pages

This optional section provides homework ideas for teachers who want or need to give more homework than is assigned to accompany the activities in this unit. The problems included here provide additional practice in learning about number relationships and in solving computation and number problems. For number units, you may want to use some of these if your students need more work in these areas or if you want to assign daily homework. For other units, you can use these problems so that students can continue to work on developing number and computation sense while they are focusing on other mathematical content in class. We recommend that you introduce activities in class before assigning related problems for homework.

Story Problems   Story problems at various levels of difficulty are used throughout the *Investigations* curriculum. The five story problem sheets provided here help students review and maintain skills that have already been taught. You can make up other problems in this format, using numbers and contexts that are appropriate for your students. Students solve the problems and then record their strategies, using numbers, words, and pictures.

Practice Page A

Kim has 4 yellow pattern blocks.
Gina has 5 green pattern blocks.
Peter has 6 red pattern blocks.
How many do they have in all?

Show how you solved this problem.
Use pictures, numbers, or words.

Practice Page B

There are 30 children in the class.
But 4 children were out sick today.
How many children were in class today?

Show how you solved this problem.
Use pictures, numbers, or words.

Practice Page C

Joey had 12 pennies.
He spent 7 of them.
Then how many did he have?

Show how you solved this problem.
Use pictures, numbers, or words.

Practice Page D

Nora has 6 storybooks at home.
She takes out 8 library books.
Now how many books does she have?

Show how you solved this problem.
Use pictures, numbers, or words.

Practice Page E

Neelam has 4 purple crayons.
George has 3 green crayons.
Pilar has 6 yellow crayons.
How many do they have in all?

Show how you solved this problem.
Use pictures, numbers, or words.